COACH
YOURSELF
Through the
AUTISM
SPECTRUM

of related interest

Autism Heroes
Portraits of Families Meeting the Challenge
Barbara Firestone, Ph.D.
Forewords by Teddi Cole and Gary Cole and Catherine Lord, Ph.D.
Photographs by Joe Buissink
ISBN 978 1 84310 837 5

Voices from the Spectrum
Parents, Grandparents, Siblings, People with Autism, and
Professionals Share Their Wisdom
Edited by Cindy N. Ariel and Robert A. Naseef
ISBN 978 1 84310 786 6

Hints and Tips for Helping Children with Autism Spectrum
Disorders
Useful Strategies for Home, School, and the Community
Dion E. Betts and Nancy J. Patrick
ISBN 978 1 84310 896 2

Fun with Messy Play
Ideas and Activities for Children with Special Needs
Tracey Beckerleg
ISBN 978 1 84310 641 8

COACH
YOURSELF
Through the
AUTISM
SPECTRUM

RUTH KNOTT SCHROEDER

Jessica Kingsley Publishers
London and Philadelphia

First published in 2009
by Jessica Kingsley Publishers
116 Pentonville Road
London N1 9JB, UK
and
400 Market Street, Suite 400
Philadelphia, PA 19106, USA

www.jkp.com

Copyright © Ruth Knott Schroeder 2009

Library of Congress Cataloging in Publication Data
Knott Schroeder, Ruth.
Coach yourself through the autism spectrum / Ruth Knott Schroeder.
  p. cm.
Includes bibliographical references and index.
ISBN 978-1-84905-801-8 (pb : alk. paper) 1. Autistic children--Family relationships.
2. Parents of autistic children. 3. Autism--Patients--Family relationships. 4. Autism in
children. 5. Child rearing. I. Title.
RJ506.A9K59 2009
618.92'85882--dc22
                    2009001271

British Library Cataloguing in Publication Data
A CIP catalogue record for this book is available from the British Library

ISBN 978 1 84905 801 8

Printed and bound in the United States by
Thomson-Shore, 7300 Joy Road, Dexter, MI 48130

For Gracey and Jordan—two most amazing people
You are my very heart

Contents

SECTION II: Parenting Neurotypical Siblings

SECTION III: Parent Care and Long-term Health

Foreword

As a young teenager, I was attracted to people with disabilities. So much so, that throughout high school, I worked in our "special needs" classroom. I loved helping the students. I got excited when an idea finally made sense. I enjoyed knowing that the students felt valued by those of us who were in the class with them. I hated it when students were teased and taunted. It seemed so unfair. They hadn't asked to be different. Like each of us, they just were.

In the summers during high school, I worked at Coyote Point, near San Mateo, CA at a summer camp for people who were physically and mentally challenged. I loved pushing their wheel chairs and talking with people who had cerebral palsy and other disabilities. We did crafts and outdoor activities near the San Francisco Bay. One summer, I worked in a private camp just for children with autism. Although it was a very challenging summer in many ways, I thought that my life work would be helping people with needs such as these.

My husband, Don, and I met in college. In 1970 after getting married and graduating, we drove to Julesburg, Colorado where we began our marriage. In Julesburg, there was a residential school for cognitive and developmentally disabled children, ages 6–18. Even though I was 20 years younger than any of the teachers, I was hired immediately as the "head teacher." Clearly the one with the least experience, I was the only one with a college degree. Thus, at age 21, I began several years of immersion into autism and other cognitive disorders.

Autism has always been an enigma to me. On the outside, those with autism can look normal. On the inside, it's a different story. As I got to know some of the children and their parents, I realized what a challenge the disorder is. I watched parents suffer because they couldn't connect the way they did with other children. I encouraged teachers who became frustrated when students didn't pay attention. I observed myself being discouraged when simple things were not so simple. It was a time of learning and teaching, discovery and disturbance, wanting to be idealistic while living in the reality of disabilities.

Fast forward thirty years. I entered the field of coaching in 1995 after finding out about it at a national mental health board meeting. I heard about coaching on a Saturday, went home on Sunday, called a coach and hired him on Monday, and had my first coaching session the next day. I was hooked. Immediately.

My learning curve with coaching was steep. In 1997, I was hired by Coach U to launch their corporate coach training programs, and in 2000 I went full time with The Ken Blanchard Companies. Toward the end of 2003, I was contacted by Dr. Norm Thiesen who is part of Western Seminary's faculty in Portland, Oregon. Norm wanted to launch a coach training program at Western. As we talked, I became excited about the prospect, knowing this would have to fit alongside my work at Blanchard. I invited a colleague, Jane Creswell, into the project, and we designed 120 hours of coach training for

Western. In June 2004 the first coaching classes were offered. Ruth Schroeder, along with several of her friends, was in those classes.

From the moment I met her, I liked Ruth. With her red hair and her outgoing personality, Ruth was an active participant in the coaching classes. During the first class, Ruth shared information about her family, particularly about her son, Jordan. Since all of the skill practices in the classes involved current challenges and opportunities, details of her life with Jordan emerged. Ruth and her fellow learners shared, practiced coaching, and very quickly the first class ended.

Toward the end of the second class, Ruth made herself vulnerable during a coaching skill practice. After the skill practice ended, it was obvious that Ruth was in turmoil. People wanted to help but didn't know how. Knowing that Ruth was walking away in pain, Jane and I ended that class. We knew that another class would start 10 days later, and we looked forward to seeing Ruth again.

Not only did she come back, but she came back joyfully. When the class began, Ruth shared about the transformation that was occurring in her life, based on the coaching and the turmoil from the previous class. She had had a breakthrough during the time between classes, and it showed on her face. Ruth glowed.

Two months later, her private practice *Cope to Hope Coaching* was launched for parents of children with autism. Since then she has published several articles in autism/Asperger's journals and magazines regarding the effectiveness of coaching with these often road-weary parents.

For Ruth, as for many of us, the past five years have been years of continuous learning, hard work, hard parenting, and hard decisions. Ruth survived. Ruth has thrived both personally and professionally as she has coached autism-impacted families around the U.S., speaking on coaching and autism, and even coach-training in a variety of contexts.

Ruth and I clearly remember having dinner one night even before Ruth engaged in the coaching classes. We were with friends, talking about coaching. When Ruth mentioned autism, it clicked that coaching would work well. The process of coaching is very effective with this demographic. In fact, that painful, turmoil-filled coaching skill practice turned out to be a watershed moment in Ruth's life.

Sharing her experiences with Jordan, with autism and with coaching others who are living with autism, Ruth offers *Coach Yourself Through the Autism Spectrum* as a gift to parents and family members who have autism in their midst. This book is based on and is for real people struggling with very real challenges. This book is full of practical insights and questions to help family members move forward, as well as tips to help deal with the trials that are part of the disorder.

As you read this book, I pray…

…..that you would be encouraged to take some of the ideas and to try them

…. that people will come to mind with whom you can network and share the journey

…that you will discover the benefits of coaching as Ruth, and her clients, and millions of others have

….that you would feel supported by the content in this book and that you would pass that support on to others, thereby lightening each other's loads.

Linda J. Miller, MA, Master Certified Coach

Acknowledgments

Thank you, Jordan Schroeder for tutoring me in the fine art of autism. Without you, I would never have discovered this remarkable world!

Gracey Schroeder, you've been given a tough job and you do it with such style.

Linda Miller, MCC, and Jane Creswell, MCC—thank you for ushering me into coaching. You were right!

Thank you to my professors at Western Seminary for the quality of education and the depth of personal support: Kay Bruce, Psy.D., Dave Wenzel, Ph.D., Gerry Breshears, Ph.D., Sandy Wilson D.Min., Norm Thiesen, Ph.D.—for "mentioning" coaching and insisting that I write.

My loving, supportive extended family: the Prante clan: my sis Janelle—our phone calls keep me sane—Zane, Jayme, Allen, Andrew, Jon. The Knott clan: my brother Paul, Betty, Jason, Melinda, Ethan, Josh, Ema, Caleb, Michelle, Cayden, Tiff, Tyler, Brianna. I'm so thankful for each one of you. To the memory of our Dad and Mom, Bert and Marian Knott who invested much in us even though their years were few.

Matt Schroeder, you're a great dad.

Connie and J.R. Baker—for your deep encouragement, life experience and Pinochle.

Reunion 6 Malachi women: Lori Davis, Joyce Schroeder, Jerri Kayll, Laura Hash, Connie Patty for 25 years of friendship (are we *really* that old?). God alone knows how our journeys have been impacted by praying together for the last 12 years.

Savory Seven women: Pam Byerley, Karen DeGraaf, Meredith Wilson, Caroline Watts, Laura Stager, Jeanie Whaley— who lived through many an "Autism in August" with me. Laughing till we cried was the best medicine.

Friends at Grace Community Church, you are just that, a grace community.

My friends at the former Columbia Counseling group: Brian Cox, LCSW, the master of humor for healing; Naomi Mandsager, Ph.D., clinical supervisor extraordinaire; Dan Cox, M.A., LPC, my coach training colleague; and MaryJane Wilt, M.A., LPC, M.A.Ed.—dear friend, fellow writer, and sojourner.

Dina Yerex, M.A., LPC for the insightful, constructive suggestions for this book. You strengthened it beyond knowing. Thank you for your investment of time.

Dave and Hollis Wenzel for your friendship, support and comedy relief.

Asperger's Professionals Group—it's great to have a "village"—Roger Meyer, Lisa Lieberman, LCSW, Peggy Piers, M.Ed. You've taught me more than you can imagine.

Portland Asperger's Partners Support Group—you guys are a highlight of my month!

My coach, friend and cheerleader Frank Skidmore—you *know* this book wouldn't have happened without you. It always starts with an impossible task.

Elsbeth Martindale, Psy.D. and the Women's Strength and Restoration Group.

My Autism Clinic friends at Oregon Health and Science University—Cheetos for everyone!

Friends and family in Haxtun, Colorado who gave me such a great start in life including my teachers Marilyn Garretson, and the memory of Gerald Jarman. This book started with their training way back in the old high school.

Most of all, thanks be to God.

Soli Deo Gloria

Preface

Coaching is a structured conversation between two people: the coach and the person being coached (PBC).

Welcome to our coaching conversation.

Pull up a chair, or a stool, or a counter and pick a chapter topic that relates to where you are at today, this moment. Or if you'd rather, read the book straight through.

The chapters are written to encourage and assure you that you are not alone as a parent of a child with autism. There are millions of us around the globe. Some of our experiences are similar and some are unique to the individual family.

A number of the vignettes are my own—I'm the single mom of an 18-year-old son with classic autism and a neurotypical* daughter age 14. Many of the stories are about parents I am privileged to know around the US who have "leaned in" to their lives by joining in the coaching process. Some are about

---

* "Autism-ese" for a person not on the autism spectrum. See the "Autism-ese" Glossary for the interpretation of a few key words and phrases used in the "world" of autism.

friends of mine in the Portland, Oregon area who amaze me at their creativity and approach to parenting.

All names and identifying information have been changed for confidentiality.

The end of each chapter provides a coaching exercise for you to focus on what *you* want to focus on, and discover an action plan that suits *you*.

Coaching is not about advice-giving or the coach telling you how to live your life.

As a coach, I believe parents are creative and resourceful.

You are the expert in your child and family.

Coaching holds a space for you to sort, discover and decide.

As the coach, I have the privilege of joining with you.

Let's start with a question I often ask PBCs…

How would you like to use our time?

—Ruth

SECTION I:

PARENTING CHILDREN
on the
AUTISM
SPECTRUM

1

Meltdowns

◇◇◇◇◇◇◇◇◇◇◇◇◇◇◇◇◇◇◇◇◇◇◇◇◇◇◇◇◇◇◇◇◇

An official dictionary definition of meltdown—1. Severe over-heating of a nuclear reactor core, resulting in melting of the core and escape of radiation. 2. A disastrous or rapidly developing situation likened to the melting of a nuclear reactor core (*American Heritage® Dictionary of the English Language* 2006).

The unofficial "Autism-ese" definition: meltdown—the sudden and sometimes unexplainable outburst or shutdown of a person impacted by autism/Asperger's. The rapidly developing situation could lead to uncontrollable crying, self-injurious behavior, complete withdrawal and/or utter parent fatigue.

Many children with autism hit bumps in the road when all their sensors have hit maximum capacity. The result may be what many parents call "a meltdown." It can look a lot of different ways: a tantrum on the floor of the grocery store, completely shutting down and using no words or gestures at a birthday party, inconsolable crying at the dinner table. Usually meltdowns happen quickly without much prior notice.

A meltdown story

Gotta love family vacations in August! Camping next to the Puget Sound in Washington State, hiking, fishing, swimming, napping—what a fun break from routine this holiday was. Jordan and Gracey hauled the water, Dad tended the fire, I planned the meals, and we all helped cook and clean up. By the end of the fourth day, an awfully grimy crew was sleeping in our camper! Definitely shower time.

The girls went first while the guys washed the dishes. Never has the simplicity of hot, spraying water felt so refreshing. Clean hair to clean feet—ahhh. Gracey and I went back to camp and tucked ourselves in the thick, blue flannel plaid of our sleeping bags. The guys headed off three-quarters of a mile away to enjoy the same hot-water luxury. Everyone in our campground quieted down in the way that cordial campers do. My quirky British novel was the perfect ending to a lovely day.

About 20 minutes later, a loud piercing scream jolted me out of my whodunit book. The novice ear might believe someone was terribly hurt. This must be an emergency of a most dramatic kind. My seasoned ear recognized it immediately: Jordan was having a meltdown.

Campers rushed to the shower house. Of course, a park ranger was called. Suspicions were raised because this disabled teenage boy was hysterically screaming while showering and the only person around was his dad.

How do you explain?

"He is severely impacted by autism."

"At home, he prefers baths to showers."

"We're out of our normal routine and somehow this was the melting point."

"The crowd pressing around is only adding to the escalation."

"Can we please just get back to our camper where he can do his bedtime routine and be comforted by the familiar?"

Meltdowns happen in the most embarrassing places—the grocery store, the restaurant, the family reunion, church, school. Meltdowns also happen at home on what I call "drawbridge days." All outside appointments and activities are canceled as we pull up the drawbridge, put the alligators in the moat, and hunker down for a low-stimulus day at home. By evening, I'm never sure who is more wrung-out, him or me.

Why do meltdowns happen? Sometimes I can retrace our steps and find the trigger. Other times, I'm as bewildered as the park ranger. One thing is for sure. If you have autism at your house, you will have meltdowns.

Coach yourself through Meltdowns

A. What was happening immediately prior to the meltdown?

1. How did the meltdown escalate and transpire?

2. What was happening two hours before?

3. The day before?

4. Taking into account all of the above information, what seems the most likely cause?

Sometimes this answer will be clear and other times completely muddy. No one can always figure it out. If you're stumped, skip the following questions and go directly to section B.

5. In future, what changes could you make earlier in the process?

6. How will you remind yourself?

7. What will you do differently next time?

Now go to section C.

B. If no reasonable cause emerges, how can you give yourself a breather to recover from the intensity of this unexpected meltdown?

C. How will you give comfort to your child?

1. How will you give comfort to your other children?

2. How will you give comfort to yourself?

3. What activity needs to be deleted from your plans today? Tomorrow?

4. What's the next thing to be done?

5. When will you do it? Date: _____ Time: _____

Ideas to take away with you

What's your "take-away" from coaching yourself through Meltdowns? *Writing it down anchors the learning.*

2
Outings

Lola's story

Lola was living a tough year. Recently divorced, back in school for her teaching credential, and parenting nine-year-old Warren with Asperger's, Lola was terribly ill with meningitis. With her hearing, balance and vision all affected, she had to go through months of therapy to regain walking and driving skills. While doing the work of a long recovery, her parenting challenges mounted. As she had been successfully coached in the academic realm, she decided to try coaching to help with parenting her autism spectrum son. (For more of Lola's story, see Chapter 19: Parent Care.)

In one session, her chosen topic was preparing for a girl's birthday party to which Warren was invited. Knowing Warren, Mom was concerned about his impulse control and boundaries regarding birthday protocol. She could just hear him saying, "Cool! Gifts and birthday cake, I get to do this!" and could foresee him helping himself by opening the girl's presents and blowing out the candles on her cake.

Through coaching, Lola devised a plan of using business-sized laminated cards. One for Warren. Three for her.

The week before the big event, she started working with him on appropriate phrases and behavior for birthday parties. His card had phrases for him to use, like, "May I sit here and watch while you open your gifts?" It also had self-talk messages for Warren to read to himself: "This is Kylie's birthday; she opens her own gifts without my help." The card was inconspicuous, small enough to fit in his pocket and hand. No one else at the party would even know he had it.

Lola's three cards were simply colors: green, yellow and red. Again, small enough not to draw attention, the cards could signal Warren across the room regarding his behavior. They both knew that green meant "You're doing well, way to go! Keep it up, Wolfie!" (his nickname). Yellow meant "Alert! Changes need to be made," and when Mom walked toward Warren with the red card, it clearly communicated "You're out of control!"

After that time, the laminated card became a staple of the Lola-Warren team. They've gone through several versions depending upon Warren's changing social needs. Now at age 12, Warren is successfully handling a variety of social situations including the local herbgrowing society, an African drumming social skills group, and many birthday parties! He now carries a laminated "security" card with every contact phone number he might need, including that of his therapist, library and the local Starbucks. *My kinda kid.*

Lola says the card which contributed most to her healthy recovery had the following words:

		May I interrupt?		
Yes	No	5	10	15

This card provided Warren with a way to ask his mom questions without disrupting. She could point to her answer indicating how long—5, 10, or 15 minutes—until she would be ready to talk with him. Of course, abuses of the interruption card had consequences— ranging from reduction of his TV time to being charged small amounts of his pocket money. To this day, she keeps this card with a flat, little timer tucked in her purse, just in case she and Warren need it.

To those who've cast doubts on her system, Lola unapologetically answers, "We as adults make grocery lists and have post-it note reminders. How is that different from an unobtrusive, laminated card?"

Lola and Warren are a courageous pair. They've faced serious challenges with grace, tenacity, and creativity. Who could have guessed so much progress could come from one mom's idea of a card in a pocket at a birthday party? She definitely had the best answer within her.

Coach yourself through Outings

1. List the outings you are concerned about.

2. Of all of these, which one do you want to focus on right now?

3. Project yourself into the future, the outing is finished and you are on your way home.

   ○ If it had gone perfectly, what would you want to have happened at this outing?

   ○ What would you want to have prevented from happening?

   ○ Which of these do you want to focus on—making something happen or stopping something happening?

4. In the past, think about one time you successfully navigated a similar outing (the idea here is to look for even a small success to learn from.)

   ○ What made it work?

5. What elements of this success can you bring to your current dilemma?

6. What preparations need to be made before the outing?

7. Which of these will you focus on?

8. When will you do it?

   Date: _____ Time: _____

9. Who can you ask for added support, encouragement, and accountability?

10. How will you celebrate when the outing is complete? (Even small successes need to be celebrated!)

11. Who will hold you accountable to make sure you celebrate?

Ideas to take away with you

What's your "take-away" from coaching yourself through Outings? Writing it down anchors the learning.

3

Childcare
and Respite

<><><><><><><><><><><><><><><><><><><><><><>

One family

Julia and Jon faced a gargantuan decision. Would they perma-
nently stay in a new city with no immediate family, no community and few friends, but one which offered appropriate autism
support for their three-year-old son Henry?

While his parents were working abroad in Germany,
Henry started losing language and eye contact at about 24
months. Concerned about his development, the family moved
stateside to what they hoped would be a temporary arrange-
ment. A year later, Henry was diagnosed with classic autism.
The county and school district services were in place and
functioning—finally!

Henry's autism was intense. Behind in his development, he
had a few words, and experienced extreme communication, behavioral, and sensory issues. Adjusting to the new experience
of having a baby sister complicated his world. The motivated
parents sought out all the information they could find and
systematically accessed resources as needed, structuring their
home systems to benefit Henry and family.

Three days a week, Julia prepared breakfast pancakes for him before the short bus (see "Autism-ese" Glossary) arrived, to help him understand the difference between a school day and a home day. Their calendar included regular appointments with speech pathologists, occupational therapists, behavioral specialists, etc. This wasn't the life they were accustomed to and the grief at times was palpable, like a direct kick to the stomach. With time they began to deal with the angst and fear of this unexpected life.

Jon and Julia longed to return to cross-cultural living in Germany. They knew they could access autism services in Europe, but the language issue was a problem. Henry was experiencing so much difficulty with American English and culture, how in good conscience could they move him to a new place and ask him to deal with an entirely different language? Another plausible option was to move nearer to extended family, but that would mean a decrease in services for Henry. With both sadness and anticipation, Jon and Julia acknowledged, "We will stay here and rebuild."

Julia describes the decision as "erasing the chalkboard" of their life and starting over. The change meant an entirely different career path for both parents, which also meant a hefty cut in pay. Julia looked for employment with flexibility for the sometimes urgent needs of her family.

Research done at The Children's Institute in Rochester, New York confirms what many autism-impacted families, including Julia and Jon, have suspected that "...autism spectrum disorder [is] associated...with higher probability that childcare problems will greatly affect employment" of parents (Montes and Halterman 2008b).

When Jon and Julia had jobs, the next challenge was daunting. What about childcare? A daycare center or private provider? In home or out of home? From the internet, they downloaded "choosing childcare checklists," from different websites to learn the best questions to ask. Many phone interviews ended prematurely as soon as Julia or Jon mentioned the "A" word—autism. They were often told, "Oh, no we can't take a child like that; we don't have the resources."

Disheartened at what seemed to be extremely limited resources, a new perspective was presented to them in the discovery of the book *A 'Stranger' Among Us: Hiring In-Home Support for a Child with Autism Spectrum Disorders or Other Neurological Differences* by Lisa Lieberman. Even from page 1, the author laid out options Julia and Jon hadn't thought of after thinking things over for hours:

A vast array of childcare options is available to families, including...

- Extended family helping in the child's home or family member's home

- Hiring a provider (outside the family) to come to the home

- Sharing an in home provider with another family

- "Stay at home" neighbor who watches your child along with own kids

- "Live-in" provider (including "au-pair" arrangements [a foreign national arrangement])

- After-school care on site

- Combination or variation of the above (Lieberman 2005, pp.1–2).

With renewed vision, the couple completed exercises in the book like "Defining Your Family Culture and Needs" (p.25), and "Clarifying Job Responsibilities" (p.37). Together, they discovered the type of person their family was looking for. Lieberman's practical step-by-step suggestions provided the structure they needed to seek, screen and eventually hire a well-suited applicant named Amy. She learned their household structure and enjoyed both Henry and his baby sister Abbey while becoming a dear friend to Julia. Now, do all in-home caregiver stories end that way? Of course not.

Eventually, Amy moved to pursue her own career. The children were seven and four, and childcare was once again a concern.

Like many autism-impacted families before them, Julia and Jon discovered that finding childcare and respite providers is a perpetual issue.

A road with potholes

When it comes to finding appropriate care for your children, I wish I could give you a nice list that would solve it for you forever. Even though we'd like to believe differently, the truth is childcare solutions are most often non-permanent. Some situations work for a long time. For example, we had an excellent in-her-home provider for years of after-school and summer care, but Jordan grew up and got too big for the smaller kids there. Some situations last for very short times, for example a young adult home from college on holiday break or a family available for one weekend.

In the autism parenting experience, this particular road is filled with "potholes." Sometimes the need is urgent and immediate, for example when Julia was starting a new job. Sometimes several potholes appear together (e.g. an-out-of-town wedding, an office holiday party, and a provider with strep throat all in the same week). Other times, the road is smooth for awhile then a chasm big enough to swallow your car opens up in front of you. At least it feels that big—like receiving a call from the daycare center stating your child with autism bit another child, must be picked up immediately and will not be allowed into the facility again.

Respite (taking an autism-free zone for parents or the rest of the family) can be even more complicated to find. I'm remembering dozens of conversations with parents over the past 15 years who at the mention of the word "respite" roll their eyes, shake their heads, sometimes saying sarcastically, "Right, where do you find someone?" or "With such a tight budget, how could we ever pay those prices? A weekend would take our whole vacation budget." Unfortunately, finding and keeping providers is an ongoing cycle.

Childcare and respite providers sometimes come from expected places—a county list of respite providers, a local provider website, an undergrad OT (see "Autism-ese" Glossary) student who sees your posting, or an extended family member. Occasionally, in odd ways, parents run across an individual who intuitively understands autism—a friend of a friend, the daughter of your hairdresser, the guy who works in your neighborhood book shop, the girlfriend of the drummer of the band your cousin sings in. Some people can be taught the basics of autism at your house and take great care of your kids.

A perpetual predicament

In writing this book, I truly wanted to have the answers for childcare and respite, even though the process of coaching is about discovering answers with the PBC rather than delivering information. My own coach called my attention to the cyclical nature of this issue. It's a bit embarrassing to admit, but I was searching for a happy ending, sure-fire formula, but there isn't one to be found. I've experienced Lisa Lieberman's book to be by far the most helpful for both in-home and out-of-home care.

As a parent, I know the discouragement and fatigue that can come with searching for appropriate help.

As a coach, I believe most parents are resourceful and creative who, with some coaching support, can make their way across the current pothole.

Coach yourself through Childcare and Respite

Not to worry about the length of the coaching exercise! It's actually set up as a "menu" with several options to choose from. Start with the first seven questions, then choose the exercise that best fits your current dilemma.

1. What current childcare/respite pothole are you facing?

2. What size is it?

3. When you've been in this predicament before, what worked to get you out of it? Even for a short time—we're not looking for a one-time fix-all.

4. How can you utilize the previous solution this time?

5. How does it need to be modified?

6. What are your known options? Write them down.

7. In your thinking, how might you be limiting yourself?

You will find two different coaching exercises below, Option 1 or Option 2. Pick one that fits your dilemma:

Option 1: coaching exercise

Now, with your permission, let's go on a discovery spree. Take three sheets of paper and write "A" on the top of the first, "B" on the second, and "C" on the third. Quickly, without stopping to evaluate if your answers are "right" or "wrong", note down in column format the answers to each of the following questions. The goal is to name as many people as possible:

1. "C" category: Who are your closest friends? Regardless of distance, name at least 3.

2. "B" category: Who are your buddies? People you enjoy, know from work, club, faith community, etc., name at least 10.

3. "A" category: Who are your acquaintances? You may or may not know their name. For example, your down-the-street neighbor with the same dog, your mail carrier, or the other runner you've had a conversation with a couple of times. Don't stop to evaluate how well you know them. If a face pops into your head, note it down. Remember, the point of this exercise is to record as many people as possible. Name at least 30.

4. To assist in getting you out of your current childcare/respite pothole, which list would you like to focus on in this session?

5. Pick one of the "C", "B" or "A" exercises below. Of course, you can always come back to the other lists at another time.

Many of us parents in autism-impacted families put on a very brave face, sometimes to our detriment because people just assume we're handling it without problems. Yikes! If they only knew.

"C" SHEET—CLOSE FRIENDS

a. How much does each of these close friends know about your life as a parent of a child with autism/Asperger's?

b. What would you like for each of them to know about your childcare/respite pothole?

c. How might they be able to support you even from a distance? (See Appendix 4: How Can I Help? which includes a coaching exercise for people who want to be supportive, but aren't quite sure how.)

d. What is the best way to communicate with each of your close friends? Example: email, phone call, letter, etc.

e. Who will you contact first?

f. When? Date: _____ Time: _____

g. When finished with this exercise, proceed to "Ideas to take away with you" section at the end of the chapter.

"B" SHEET—BUDDIES

a. Which of these buddies knows you have a child with autism/Asperger's?

b. Which of these buddies would you like to know you have a child with autism/Asperger's?

c. How might you tell them?

d. Which ones do you want to know about your child-care/respite dilemma?

e. What information might they know that could be helpful to you? Example: "We're looking for an occasional caregiver after school. Do you know of any college students who might be interested?" Of course, from here, you would conduct an in-depth interview, background check, etc.

f. Which ones might know other people who could possibly be a resource?

g. What are you going to do?

h. When? Date: _____ Time: _____

i. When finished with this exercise, proceed to "Ideas to take away with you" section at the end of the chapter.

"A" SHEET—ACQUAINTANCES

a. Which of these acquaintances know you are the parent of a child with autism/Asperger's?

b. What information might your acquaintances know that could be helpful to you?

c. Which ones might know other people who could possibly be a resource?

d. What are you going to do?

e. When? Date: _____ Time: _____

f. When finished with this exercise, proceed to "Ideas to take away with you" section at the end of the chapter.

Option 2: Alternate coaching exercise

Answer the following questions by quickly writing down any organizations that come to mind. Don't get caught up in evaluating your answers; write down the first things that come to mind:

1. What colleges and universities are within 25 miles of your home?

2. What university hospitals are within 25 miles of your home?

3. What alternative medicine training centers are within 25 miles of your home?

4. Who might you contact at these institutions for posting your childcare/respite request?

5. What organizations do you belong to? Example: community club, chamber of commerce, faith community, etc.

6. Who in these organizations is in charge of member care or resource management?

7. What information might this person know that could be helpful to you?

8. What community organizations are active in your community? Example: Kiwanis, Lions Club, Rotary Club, etc.

9. What information might they have that could be helpful to your situation?

10. What businesses offer childcare/respite for families with special needs?

11. On the internet, what blog sites offer helpful information?

12. What autism organizations are in your state, county, province, township, etc.?

13. Of all these organizations, which one will you contact first? Second? Third?

14. What will you do? When?

Date: _____ Time: _____

Ideas to take away with you

What's your "take-away" from coaching yourself through Childcare and Respite? Writing it down anchors the learning.

4

Doctor Visits

Can you imagine? What would it be like?

Walking into a strange room, being expected to sit on a table higher than your head covered in what feels like sand paper with horribly loud crunching sounds in your ears? With a strobe light blinking above, you're already feeling ill when a strange person in a bright, white coat sweeps in and pokes long, hard, cold instruments in your ears and nose. This person expects you to open your mouth and be prodded with a wooden stick longer than your hand! The unfamiliar, cold hands poke around your stomach, pushing here and there. Not only that, but your mom or dad is actually holding you down, not helping you escape from this strange tormenter! Utter betrayal.

If you had limited language, what would you do?

Answer: I'd scream, clamp my mouth shut, kick and flail until everybody left me alone.

Going to the doctor can be trauma for kids with autism.

The year of illness

Like many families, when my kids were just starting school, we had a year of constant illness. We're not just talking about the gooey cold here and there. I mean full fledged bronchitis, multiple sinus infections, and the "best" part of all, good old-fashioned influenza. Once our resistance was down, every other germ that happened to be floating through the air took hold and had a party. Months of it. On occasion, friends would bring us dinner, leaving it on our doorstep. If a ten-foot pole had been handy, I bet they would have used it to push the foodstuffs toward our door. No one wanted to enter the Schroeder Infirmary for fear of what they might catch. Ever had a year or years like that?

Nine at the time, Jordan got hit hardest with flu—the real flu, not just the upset tummy flu. After going to the doctor's office three times in three days for constant diarrhea and vomiting, he stopped drinking and ended up in a local children's hospital with dehydration.

He was so scared and so sick, not understanding why strangers were sticking needles in him. The worst for me, the mom, was when they put the needle in his hand through which they would give him liquids intravenously. He wanted it out and wanted it out now. For a boy with severe sensory issues the procedure must have felt cruel. Jordan really was brave; he actually adjusted and left it alone.

Some of the doctors and students on rounds were extremely kind and gentle—I suspect those are the ones who actually read his chart before entering the room. It's fascinating that the most inexperienced student doctors seemed the smuggest. For those who arrogantly waltzed in, I was definitely like the mama bear. Standing up to my tallest five feet nine inches and raising the hair on my neck, I filled the space between the door and the hospital bed. If they hadn't read the chart, I informed them of the entire health history including a small lecture on autism before they could get within four feet of my son.

A few days and countless bags of IV fluids later, we both went home exhausted and thankful for the familiar.

How do we as parents advocate for our children when they're ill? The question is particularly daunting when often we are sick ourselves or getting sick or just recovering from being sick. It can be tricky for us parents to tell the difference between a situation in which we are looking for different responses from the medical staff as opposed to one in which everything may have been done as well as possible and yet the child still has difficulty. It may surprise you to learn that we autism-impacted parents have a reputation for being demanding and uncooperative.

My personal motto has been, "You catch more bees with honey than with vinegar." Meaning, if I am pleasant, collaborative and kind, I'm more likely to build a team who really wants to help my son. When goodwill is established, I get a lot more of what I want for my son. On the other hand, there are times—like with the student doctors in the hospital—when it was time to let my internal "steel" show.

In the medical world, some doctors "get it" and some just don't. Dr. Egens the pediatrician got it. He turned out the harsh overhead lighting, took off his white coat and even allowed his young patients to play on his computer while checking them out. Sadly, our insurance changed and we had to switch health care practitioners.

A family physician, Dr. Knopf educates his staff on the needs of autism-impacted families. Spectrum folks are accommodated with shorter wait times, compassionate nurses, and an appreciation of how invasive and offensive a check-up can be for someone with sensory issues. Their kindness will never be forgotten, especially the year before our trip to the hospital when neon-yellow stomach fluids projectiled all over the treatment room!

Coach yourself through Doctor Visits

1. What information does your child need to know before going to the doctor? Example: "First, car ride, then waiting room, then treatment room," etc.

2. What is the most effective way of communicating information to your child? Example: picture schedule, social story, checklist, video, etc.

3. How far in advance does your child need to receive this information?

4. In what setting does your child best incorporate new information? Example: sitting on a beanbag in her room, on your lap after a story, at the table, etc.

5. What comfort items will your child need to take along to soothe himself? Example: favorite blanket, Thomas the Tank Engine toys, weighted vest, etc.

6. What reward can your child receive for a job well done? Never underestimate the value of positive reinforcers. (Most people, including children, respond to positive encouragement with positive behavior. I sure know I respond much more positively to praise and reward than I do to criticism and punishment.)

7. What reward will *you* receive for braving the doctor's office? *Never underestimate the value of celebrating your own accomplishments!*

8. How much recovery time will you and your child need after the appointment?

9. What will you and your child do during this recovery time?

10. What changes need to be made in today's schedule to accommodate a doctor's visit?

Ideas to take away with you

What's your "take-away" from coaching yourself through Doctor's Visits? Writing it down anchors the learning.

5

"Invisible" Autism—
the Unique Isolation of
"High Functioning"

"Invisible" autism brings a silent ache which is carried by many parents. The painful pattern starts at first with the high-functioning child coming across as typical to acquaintances, teachers and even family members. If the child acts out just a bit or starts relating in a less than typical manner, the differences are often attributed to "bad parenting" with raised-eyebrow messages aimed directly at the parents. Hidden autism/Asperger's can be excruciatingly tough.

In his excellent book *The Complete Guide to Asperger's Syndrome* Tony Attwood (2007) credits a 1981 study (DeMyer, Hingtgen and Jackson 1981) as the first to use the term high-functioning autism to describe children "who, as they developed, were shown in formal testing of cognitive skills to have a greater degree of intellectual ability, with greater social and adaptive behavior skills and communication skills, than is usual with children with autism" (p.44). Some kids impacted by autism/ Asperger's have some really great skills set. *Yea! That's good news to celebrate.* The difficulty lies in the interpretations of others when they bump into the unexpected areas which aren't so skilled.

Amy and AJ

At first meeting, AJ seems the same as most other boys of his age. His Asperger's isn't an obvious quirkiness, but more of a general "not-getting-it" that frustrates teachers, peers, family members and counselors. For years Amy knew something was up with her son, but couldn't put her finger on it. Spending many sleepless nights, she ruminated, wondering what was going on and how she could help. When AJ hit second grade, she suggested the possibility of autism spectrum to the school, but this was immediately discounted by the teacher and special education specialist. Finally, in fourth grade the disparity between him and his peers had widened enough for the Asperger's to be seen more clearly by his educational team and AJ was officially diagnosed at age nine. (Read more of Amy and AJ's story in Chapter 8: Sleeplessness.)

Because of Amy's challenging, high-energy, talkative, 1001-ideas son, people seem scared to offer help, resulting in Amy feeling even more isolated and alone. Yes, being around AJ is taxing, but Amy longs for someone to offer some respite. The gaps in AJ's social abilities can look like defiance to others and is perceived as the result of poor parenting. This makes people pull away from Amy. "It's a lonely life," she says quietly, without self-pity.

Coach yourself through "Invisible" Autism

1. What's the truth about your child?

2. What characteristics do other people see in your child that might make them think she or he is neurotypical?

3. What do *you* know that outsiders don't know?

4. As a parent, what are 10 things at which you excel?

5. As a parent, what are 10 things at which you excel that no one else sees?

6. What's the truth about your parenting?

7. Write at least one positive statement about your parenting ability. Example: "The structure I provide at home is her safety net." Or "She does so well at school because of the hard work we do at home." Or "I know my child better than anyone and I parent in the way she needs."

8. How will you remind yourself of what is true? Example: a sticky note on your bathroom mirror, a small card on your car dashboard, a reminder on your PDA.

9. When will you put this reminder in place?

    Date: _____ Time: _____

Ideas to take away with you

What's your "take-away" from coaching yourself through "Invisible" Autism? Writing it down anchors the learning.

6

Parenting Your Child's Strengths (Children with Autism Spectrum Disorder)

Josh—a most interesting young man

I wish you could meet Josh. He is a most interesting 19-year-old young man, with a lot to say. Like many people with autism, he developed typically until age two, then lost all of his language. *Raise your hand with me if you can relate to this!* This was back in the "good" old days when many practitioners didn't use the "A" word with parents ("A"=autism). The family doctor told Josh's mom Carollee "a lot of kids regress" and "let's just wait to let him catch up." Thankfully, now we know any type of regression is a flashing red light on the dashboard of life saying "Get this child evaluated for Autism Spectrum Disorder *immediately!*"

In preschool, Josh grew unresponsive to his name. Finally at the age of four he was diagnosed with autism. Like so many moms, Carollee scoured the area for resources with the main goal of helping him communicate. It took some work to find a medical doctor who suited Josh and Carollee, but in the

end she found a practitioner 20 miles away who was a marvel-
ous fit.

Josh's fascination with garage doors started at age five or six
and according to Mom he drew them in "gross detail." He illus-
trated dozens of garage doors of all colors and shapes including
the "springs, latches and casings." Wisely, Carollee recognized
garage doors as Josh's "connection to the world." Amazing, isn't
it how the mom's intuition is almost always right?

Educators at Josh's elementary school were frustrated with
his distractibility. Across the street from the school was a warehouse with a huge, rolling garage door. Josh couldn't possibly
concentrate on schoolwork with such a temptation just outside
the window!

Carollee's idea? Instead of trying to extinguish the "unwanted" behavior, engage his interest in garage doors in order
to teach him.

It was a risk. The educational team was unconvinced. Mom
had to do some serious advocating. With skepticism, the faculty agreed to try the experiment. His teacher started using the
garage door across the street as a learning tool. Adults and kids
began talking with Josh about garage doors, and he learned
reciprocal language skills. As a reward for work well done,
he earned trips with the school counselor to visit the garage
door.

Over the next four years, he learned practical math with
items stored in the warehouse. Josh put pen to paper on the
subject of garage doors and learned to write. His art projects
included constructing a garage door out of Popsicle® sticks and
many other creations all around the same theme. On his own,
he designed and built a folding small-scale garage door out of
wood with a pulley. Later, he built a bigger one, complete with
latches and screws.

Regarding the educational decision, Carollee declares with great satisfaction: "It *did* work." It worked so well in fact, that the garage door became a famous conversation piece around the entire school. Other kids asked why only Josh got to see it, providing a golden opportunity for him to make verbal and written invitations to other students to visit the garage door. Carolee says, "The garage door simply became 'huge' in the school and especially in Josh's inclusive classroom."

Another developing interest was commercial dishwashers. Throughout Josh's elementary, middle school and high school years, he worked in every school cafeteria, learning to interact with kitchen staff and doing what he loved—washing dishes!

In Grade 6, Josh rode around the family neighborhood on his adaptive bike, collecting materials for recycling and looking at the garage doors. Mom Carollee recognized this as another opportunity. She jogged alongside for three years. The first 18 months she directed the conversations and brokered the connection between neighbor and son. The second 18 months she asked neighbors to direct questions to Josh. Through these many trips Josh made acquaintance with most of the neighborhood, noticed anything broken on garage doors and gave sound mechanical repair advice. He still collects recycling and does garage door consultations independently.

Carollee knew her son had mechanical aptitude and gave him a wide area in the home "to make a mess and create." In middle school his interest honed in on a backyard shed. Josh and his dad insulated it, added a heater, a washer and dryer. Eventually Josh installed an air-conditioning unit and a fully wired alarm system with fire extinguishers—another passion. For his 16th birthday, instead of a car, Josh was given a shiny, beautiful commercial dishwasher which he promptly installed in his shed. Every evening to his delight, he busses out the family dishes and runs them through making sure his mom knows the number of loads it takes to finish.

Sneakily, his parents have been teaching him job skills for years. They wanted him to learn that his interests could become paying jobs as an adult. For three and a half years he worked as a dishwasher in a restaurant, starting out with Mom as a job coach, and eventually working completely independently.

Now Josh enjoys three jobs, one at a local university hospital checking fire extinguishers and alarms, volunteering at a local daycare center and installing garage doors—his own business. Every employer and customer praises his abilities, thoroughness and work ethic.

His latest accomplishment? In less than 24 hours, installing a perfectly working, hefty, rolling garage door, start to finish in his shed—and he did it all by himself.

I wish you could meet Josh. He is a most interesting 19-year-old young man, with a lot to say.

Coach yourself through Parenting Your Child's Strengths—(Children with ASD)

If your child's skill level isn't as high as Josh's, stories like the one above can feel like a knife in the belly. My son Jordan, for example, in addition to autism is severely cognitively disabled and has not and will not reach the point of independence and work opportunities which Josh is enjoying. Every child's abilities are different. Regardless of the level of impairment, his or her special interest(s) can give clues to making connections with the world. I'll tell you, studying my son's interests has provided a gold mine of learning tools which otherwise would have been missed.

1. What special interest(s) does your child have? If more than one, list them.

2. Pick one interest to focus on in this session.

3. What characteristics of this interest can be used to teach your child? Example: a child interested in trains might do better with a horizontal picture schedule.

4. "Study" the interest. What else do you notice?

5. What is it about the interest that might be so captivating? Example: sensory, color or sound.

6. How can you join your child in his or her interest to encourage communication and connection?

7. What does this interest tell you about your child?

8. How can you use this interest to impact your child's learning today? This week? At school?

9. Who will you talk to about using this interest to assist your child?

10. What will you do? Date: _____ Time: _____

Ideas to take away with you

What's your "take-away" from coaching yourself through Parenting Your Child's Strengths (Children with ASD)? Writing it down anchors the learning.

7

Educational
Decisions

◇◇◇◇◇◇◇◇◇◇◇◇◇◇◇◇◇◇◇◇◇◇◇◇◇◇◇◇◇◇◇

Many people with autism/Asperger's struggle with transitions. Many of their parents do too, perhaps even more so.

When living through the transition of major educational decisions, most parents get anxious. Some of us jump in and over-function, trying to control every person and every situation that might possibly face our child. *Uh, that would be me!* The upside is we say everything that is bothering us, feel better afterward, and appropriate changes probably happen. The downside is we may alienate ourselves from the very people who are most able to help our child. Don't get me wrong, some situations are absolutely unworkable and extreme measures must be taken.

Conversely, some parents freeze up with anxiety, unsure of how to start an "unpleasant" or "un-positive" conversation with teachers. The upside is educators don't experience the parent as uncooperative, overbearing or bossy. The downside is their reticence may delay the child from receiving timely, appropriate changes in her or his educational plan.

Every country, state, county, city, burg, township, school and classroom brings its distinctive challenges. As a child grows in wisdom and stature, their educational needs change. Keeping up with the adjustments and making proper modifications is a perpetual challenge for parents. Many ask themselves, "How and when do I make suggestions to teachers? How can I be collaborative without getting walked on?"

A family's story

"I work a lot from my intuition. I trust my gut. I definitely have grown," says Heidi six years after their son's initial diagnosis.

When two-year-old George was diagnosed, Heidi and Dan rapidly researched every angle of autism they could find. Immediately they enrolled him in the Texas state services birth-to-three program and started private occupational and speech therapy. They tried the structure of discreet trials, but it just wasn't a good fit for George or his parents. Other methods of "joining" the child to his world more closely fitted with their philosophy of following the child's lead; it just wasn't structured enough for their easily distracted boy.

In the best sense of the word, Heidi is...well...a "bulldog." One of her greatest strengths is making a plan and efficiently executing it to completion. She will not let go until she has a workable solution and finishes it! Earlier in life, her tenacity saw her through medical school and a psychiatry residency.

After hours of researching autism, she learned about a program that could be carried out entirely in the home. The principles of keeping a loving, non-judgmental attitude resonated with her and Dan. Heidi's intuition whispered, "this model will work," so she decided to listen to her gut. The program was expensive and very time-consuming, but it fit George. After weeks of training to take on the full-time role and responsibility of all of George's education and treatment, she launched the program. Managing it was more than a full-time job.

No longer practicing medicine, Heidi trained volunteers and paid staff to work with George. She managed his care including diet, medications and supplements. Literally from morning till night, she was on-duty with this rigorous program. She believed strongly in the technique of *joining* used in the model as a way to create a deep and meaningful connection with her child, built on a foundation of trust and respect. The plan provided her with the tools she needed to look again at her child in a hopeful and positive light.

When worn out, she would tell herself, "You don't *have* to do this, you could stop right now." Her reply to herself was inevitably, "But I *want* to do this. It's very important to me!" The change in attitude gave her the needed strength to keep going.

Running it all became more overwhelming with the arrival of baby brother Dominic. Having no other professionals involved, Heidi increasingly felt the sheer magnitude of George's program, saying, "I felt completely responsible for his care." Having two children divided her time.

At a crucial juncture, Heidi suddenly found herself personally depleted at a time when several key staff members had left George's program. Unsure of what to do next, she decided to see this as a sign that maybe it was time to start branching out and expanding George's world beyond just his home-based program. She began to consider the idea of sending George to school for the first time at the age of six, but felt a great deal of anxiety about the process and needed some support. That's when she called a coach.

Falling into her habit of taking a positive attitude, she quickly changed her perspective from problem to opportunity. In her coaching sessions, she developed a systematic plan of research. In the true "Heidi style" of getting a wide breadth of information, she talked to the school, contacted her local

Autism Society and called every autism contact she could find in the city of Austin.

In her community and with the degree of George's limitations, it looked as though public schools were her only option. She remained uneasy about the decision and wondered if they would try to force on George a new way of being and learning? Would they respect his limits? How much of a voice would she have? After all she was accustomed to running the whole program.

The first step was testing out at the school. George liked it, and even asked to go back! Good sign. Heidi met with the school telling them a lot about the program and the attitudes behind it. Six-year-old George started off with two mornings per week, gradually increasing hours spent at school.

In retrospect, Heidi reports, "I kind of went overboard...not in a 'mean' way, just a concerned way." She "didn't burn any bridges," and began to relax when she saw how the teacher genuinely cared about George. Heidi calls herself, "more diplomatic now," saying "[The over-functioning] came from my own anxiety and stress." *I ask you: who hasn't felt that way?*

Six years after George's diagnosis, Heidi expresses a quiet confidence, "I'm happy with the choices I've made along the way. I wouldn't change a thing."

What does Heidi recommend to parents?

- Don't hesitate to bring up concerns.

- Interact with the teacher.

- Encourage the use of rewards rather than punishment with your child.

- Don't make your only communication about the negative things. Ninety nine percent of what happens is really positive. Express your feelings about the good stuff and thank the team regularly for believing in your child. That way when the 1 percent happens and you need to challenge something, the relationship is already strong.

- Donate snacks.

- Volunteer.

- Give them thank you cards and pictures of your child as a way of strengthening your relationship with them.

- Give and request regular feedback.

- Use email, it's quick, easy and effective.

Other principles to be gained from Heidi's story:

- Listen to your intuition; it has a lot to say.

- Study your child.

- Sometimes small adjustments are needed in an educational program.

- Sometimes major changes are needed in an educational program.

- Build relationships with all of your child's caregivers.

- Be mindful of your own anxiety—we all have it! Does it drive you to over-function or freeze you up into non-action?

Most importantly:

Utilize the programs that work for *your child*. After all, you as the parent are the expert on your unique child.

Coach yourself through Educational Decisions

1. What are your current concerns about your child's education? Just write them down without thinking about the pros and cons. At this point we're only naming them.

2. Which concern is keeping you up at night?

3. Which concern do you want to focus on right now?

4. Where are you stuck?

5. Picture yourself six months into the future. How do you envision this concern to be solved or changed?

6. Go backwards and "watch" how you solved it. In reverse order, what steps did you take? (5.____ 4.____ 3.____ 2.____ 1.____)

7. What information is missing now?

8. Where can you go or who can you contact to get the missing information? When will you do this?

   Date: _____ Time: _____

9. What's the next step?

10. You *can* do this. When? Date: _____ Time: _____

11. How will you congratulate yourself for making this first step?

Ideas to take away with you

What's your "take-away" from coaching yourself through Educational Decisions? Writing it down anchors the learning.

8

Sleeplessness

AJ—the boy who doesn't sleep

AJ with Asperger's is high energy—to say the least. He's got a multitude of creative ideas swirling around in his head and wants to tell you about them all at once. Social groups with AJ are always a full-on sprint! He wants to make and keep friends more than anything, but really struggles with relationships. (Read more of AJ's story in Chapter 5: "Invisible" Autism.

AJ is also a talented artist. Really talented. His cartoons, animals, people, reality, fantasy are utterly amazing. At age ten, he is high energy about his art. Mom Amy reports drawing to be the very thing that keeps AJ from falling asleep at night. He has so much to draw and must get it "all out of his brain" before sleeping and perseverates with worry on the possibility of forgetting what it was he wanted to draw.

This sleeping problem isn't new, however. From the day he was born, literally, AJ wouldn't sleep unless his mom held him "super tight" to her chest. He had to be swaddled up securely and held tight or he just wouldn't sleep. This went on for years and Mom was beyond exhausted. Finally one day as a pre-schooler, he simply decided to go into his room and nap. That was the first time in his life he had fallen asleep on his own.

Now this isn't because Amy hadn't tried. Oh, my how she tried. Not the indulgent, coddling type of mom, she avidly read all the books about getting babies on schedules. The let-him-cry-himself-to-sleep-in-his-crib method, and many more were valiantly attempted, but AJ simply *would not* sleep. He didn't sleep much then. And he doesn't sleep much now.

Many autism-impacted families face this problem. The child does not require much sleep and consequently the parents are relentlessly sleep-deprived. A 2008 study states that, "the prevalence of sleep related complaints…is reported to be as big as 83.3% in children with autism spectrum disorders." (Ming *et al.* 2008). Because of AJ's sleeplessness, Amy reports experiencing the following results of her own sleep deprivation over the past ten years:

- "I never feel quite normal."

- "I'm a horrible coffee addict."

- "I'm on edge."

- "I don't feel like myself, like I don't have the strength to *be* myself."

- "I'm kind of a shell."

- "All of my energy goes toward being mom."

- "Where did *I* go?"

- "I know that taking care of myself is important, but when? At 4:00a.m.? That's the only time I could possibly be alone."

Amy lives with an ongoing strain on her relationship with husband and parents who "don't understand what's going on." She is told, "You need to learn to relax," but that is so tough when all she can do is pray for strength to get through the next hour, let alone the remainder of the day. The raging exhaustion remains.

Coach yourself through Sleeplessness

1. How many sleep hours does your child usually get per night?

2. How many sleep hours are you getting?

3. How is sleep deprivation impairing your child's life?

4. How is sleep deprivation impairing your life?

5. How might regular, good sleep enhance your child's life?

6. How might regular, good sleep enhance your life?

7. Which of the following brings the greatest challenge?

    ○ falling asleep

    ○ staying asleep

    ○ early morning waking.

8. Of all the things you've tried, what has worked even once?

9. What can you learn from this one success?

10. How can you provide more of it for your child?

One of the very complex aspects of chronic sleep deprivation is difficulty making decisions or thinking creatively for new options. If about now in the coaching exercise, you're feeling absolutely stuck, try turning to Chapter 11: Stuck Spots.

11. Where could you go for information on sleep hygiene? Example: Your local Autism Society, local support group.

12. How will you know it's time to seek outside help?

13. Who do you know to consult with about sleep issues? Example: medical doctor, naturopathic doctor, autism consultant.

14. What is one thing you will do differently this week regarding sleeplessness?

15. When will you do it? Date: _____ Time: _____

As a coach and a parent, I want to encourage you that there are options even if it feels like there are none. You aren't alone; millions of parents like you are aching for sleep and suffering from raging exhaustion. Take courage.—Ruth

9

Extended Family

◇◇◇◇◇◇◇◇◇◇◇◇◇◇◇◇◇◇◇◇◇◇◇◇◇◇◇◇◇◇◇◇◇◇◇◇

Above Steamboat Springs, Colorado, three tent trailers parked within 100 yards of each other. Enough distance to have both privacy and quick access. My extended family hadn't been around Jordan (age eight) for awhile. Now that he was older and differences were more and more evident, how would they *be* with him? Could we relax?

I'm not sure why I was worried. They were great. In true Knott/Prante style, every aunt, uncle and cousin moved toward Jordan in their own way. Uncle Paul spun him round and round while Jordan schooled him in Veggie Tales dialogue. Jayme, Tiff, Brianna and youngest cousin Gracey all braided their hair alike. Andrew and Jon looked out for Jordan's safety and alerted us about any concerns. Big cousins Jason, Josh and Caleb tirelessly lugged him around, hiked and high-fived for days on end.

Several meals turned into a sort of Autism 101 class with me teaching them about the basics if Autism Spectrum Disorder and how our family was impacted by it. My extended family drank it in. Of course, Jordan's diet and table manners were not like others, but in this setting, his brand of etiquette was warmly accepted.

The sadness for me is that we still live over 1200 miles away and times together are infrequent. They love Jordan and check into him, but we just aren't together much. What I appreciate most is they take initiative with him, believing that he wants to connect but he just doesn't know how.

Extended families respond to autism in different ways. (See Table opposit)

No doubt most extended families have a common thread: sadness that your life is impacted by autism, and the difficulty that brings you. They also may have a private, personal grief of their own. Autism brings loss to everyone in the family. As a child grows up, most family members grieve in different ways over the child they dreamed of having. (For more on grandparenting and supportive community see Appendices 1 and 4.)

Autism also brings *blessing*, to your immediate family, your extended family and the far reaches of your community. Some families look for support where they can find it: faith community, neighbors, friends, groups, clubs, etc. No matter the response of your extended family. Your children are a blessing—each one.

Some extended family styles

Type of extended family	Characteristics	Autism-impacted family's possible response
Daily supporters	Are those who live near you, run errands, provide respite, and know your children well.	Those of you who have this kind of support are probably grateful beyond words—how wonderful! Supportive family is the ideal. Sadly, in my American culture the solidarity of extended family is most often absent.
Distance supporters	Like my family, they probably live farther away. Perhaps they know some aspects of your life, but might be surprised by the day-to-day intensity. They give support by phone calls, email, occasional visits, etc.	Response can be gratefulness, and perhaps a sense of loss, wishing they could be more involved in daily life.
Try-to-be helpers	In town or out, they try to help, but just may not understand what works and what doesn't.	Response to this might be frustration, anger and feeling deeply alone.

Type of extended family	Characteristics	Autism-impacted family's possible response
Fixers	Often say, "I found this article and here's what you need to do to fix Aiden."	Well, thanks…but… uh… Not every autism "cure" on TV works for every child. Response can be defensiveness toward the onslaught and a need for more space from extended family. Possibly a sense of grief and deep wondering why can't my family just love and accept Aiden the way he is?
Curious onlookers	Aren't sure what to do or even how to express their desire to help. May make statements like, "Aiden is such a sweetie" without really knowing him.	Response can be mixed. May be grateful for the enjoyment, but also disappointed that more initiative isn't taken.
Pull-awayers	May be afraid of making your child "more autistic" or afraid that something they do might irretrievably push your child into his own world.	Response is often anger, sadness and a feeling of rejection. May contribute to a feeling of isolation.
Disapprovers	May communicate overt or implicit disapproval over the way you are raising your child. May blame the autism/ Asperger's on you or your spouse.	Response is often anger, resentment and shame. Perhaps you find yourself attempting to prove the disability is not your or your spouse's fault.

Coach yourself through Extended Family

1. What style(s) most closely describe(s) your extended family?

2. What are some things you'd like for them to know about your child, your family or autism in general? List at least 10.

3. Of all the things you've just written down, which one do you want to focus on?

4. How is the best way to communicate with your extended family? (Example: email, phone call, casual conversation, etc.)

5. Which family members do you anticipate communicating with easily?

6. Which family members do you anticipate more difficulty communicating with?

7. Where are you going to start?

8. What are you going to tell them?

9. When will you do it? Date: _____ Time: _____

10. What could stop you?

11. Who can cheer you on in communicating this important information?

Ideas to take away with you

What's your "take-away" from coaching yourself through **Extended** Family? Writing it down anchors the learning.

10

Bullying

◇◇◇◇◇◇◇◇◇◇◇◇◇◇◇◇◇◇◇◇◇◇

Bullying: the very word can make a parent's blood run cold.

While working as family representative in a diagnostic autism clinic, I had the sobering privilege of sitting in with doctors as they gave parents the news of an autism/Asperger's diagnosis. Remembering our family's negative experience, I was determined to offer connection and an emotional "holding" for parents to respond in any way needed.

With tears and sighs, most often the parents expressed concern for the future regarding how their child would be treated: "I don't want her/him to be made fun of" or "ridiculed" or "bullied." Words frequently followed by the question, "Will s/he have friends?"

Most of us parents experience this fear by groaning too deep for words.

What is bullying?

Dr. Tony Attwood (2007, p.96) describes bullying as including three components:

1. a power imbalance

2. intent to harm (physically or emotionally)

3. a distressed target.

Bullying often takes place where adults aren't close by, like on buses, in hallways and sports situations. It can also happen near or in a child's home by neighborhood kids, friends of the family or siblings (older or younger). Yes, a power imbalance can be in play even with a younger neurotypical sibling or friend who has learned how to get a reaction out of an older child.

In our family, my son who is severely impacted by autism experienced bullying by a six-year-old who discovered how to "push" 12-year-old-Jordan's "buttons." The Sunday School teacher noticed it when this scrawny little boy kicked my big broad-shouldered son making him cry uncontrollably. I was called out of service and recognized immediately that mostly it was Jordan's feelings that were hurt. We learned that the boy had been following him around in class for a few weeks with quiet tormenting. Didn't take long before we changed churches.

Luke—the proactive target

Ten-year-old Luke with Asperger's desperately desires friends. His difficulty with friendship skills makes him what Attwood calls a "proactive bullying target" (2007, p.99). Because of Luke's social difficulties classmates and adults interpret his underdeveloped social initiations as being intrusive and irritating (Attwood 2007, p.99). Luke wants to have friends so desperately, he gets in their face (literally), seeks attention by provoking people and trys to dominate activities. The rejection he feels is traumatizing.

Luke is a big, somewhat athletic, very competitive guy, who, as his parents describe, "doesn't know when to quit." In Phys Ed class, he has a reputation for throwing his weight around, laughing about knocking people over and loudly taunting when his team scores a goal. Of course, he hasn't understood it as bad sportsmanship. To him, it's just celebrating. More than anything, he wants to be part of a group of guys in his class. His non-malicious, earnest desire nearly got him kicked out of school for good.

True to form, Luke decided one day he would make his move by joining the daily noon recess soccer game. Walking up to the circle of popular boys, he announced in his rather high-pitched, loud voice he was going to play with them that day. The guys looked around at each other rolling their eyes and smirking. Unfortunately, Luke misinterpreted their body language and believed they were genuinely happy to include him.

Gaining confidence, in his squeaky voice, he earnestly asked the question which had been burning inside him, "Will you be my friends?" Several in the group burst out laughing. Some stood silently, but one guy, Thomas, placed his hand on Luke's shoulder saying quite sarcastically, "Of *course* we'll be your 'friends.'" All the boys understood his meaning except Luke who was thinking, "Wow that was easy, all I had to do was ask," and euphoria set in. He belonged to a group!

It was a set up. Little did Luke know, because of his trusting nature, eagerness to be a part of a group and social naïveté, he had just placed a target on his own back. Within two minutes, the torment began.

It started with name-calling like "retard" and "weirdo." Big guys body-checked and knocked him over, smaller guys intentionally kicked him, keeping the ball away from Luke until he cried. Still believing these boys were his friends because they said they were, he remained optimistic, tromping out to the playing field every day for weeks. Teachers were glad to see Luke finally being included and didn't notice the ongoing abuse out on the far playing field.

On a particularly rough day, through tears Luke reported his injuries to a playground-duty teacher who suggested Luke should "just deal with it and ignore those guys" reassuring him "everyone gets hurt playing soccer sometimes." Taking his classmates' ridicule literally, he pondered, "Maybe I really am a 'psycho.'" At home, his parents noticed he was not his usual talkative self, more quiet and withdrawn. His folks are refreshingly candid and later reported actually feeling relief to have a break from the never-ending narrative about insects, dinosaurs and time travel. *OK, now honestly, who's been there as a parent? Yeah, I thought so—me too.*

The playground tension came to a head when one minute before the bell a strategically thrown elbow from Thomas broke Luke's glasses and bloodied his nose. Walking into the school, the bully whispered a crass comment and Luke grabbed him by the neck, threw him up against the wall and started punching. Thomas received immediate attention from both adults and peers for being attacked by "that psycho kid." As described by Attwood (2007), "When the child with Asperger's syndrome retaliates with anger to…provocation, perhaps causing damage or injury, the covert 'operative' appears to be the innocent victim and receives compensation from the supervising adult" (pp.97–98). Yep, Thomas, the covert operative bully, was the hero (and the "victim") of the day.

As you might imagine, immediately Luke was escorted to the principal's office and expelled for three days.

Sophie—the passive target

Sophie dreaded the bus ride. It was OK on days when that "ratty little Neal guy" wasn't riding. But if he was there, it was miserable. The snows of Minnesota prolonged the trips which also prolonged the agony.

It was the incessant questions that bugged her and Neal knew it. He and a few other kids would gather around her seat and ask her questions. If she changed spots, Neal subtly moved to continue the barrage. Their voices were quiet for which the bus driver was grateful.

Was this really bullying? The power imbalance was Neal's verbal skills and the number of kids surrounding Sophie. Their intent was clear: to bring embarrassment, emotional discomfort and harm. She was definitely a distressed target, trying to avoid the uncomfortable attention and ruminating over the "idiotic" things that were said to her. Sophie was advised by her parents to "just ignore him" but the myth of ignoring doesn't work. "The bully will escalate his or her actions until the child responds." (Attwood 2007, p.108)

When she finally conceded and told the group of kids her favorite movie was a French flick with sub-titles, the whole group melted into laughter. Even months later, she shakes her head wondering what was so funny, "They haven't even seen it."

Nathan

Nathan both dreaded and needed recess. After all the time spent working in groups he required a quiet, solitary place to refuel. His favorite spot was a large tree at the corner of the playground. Here, he could take his squishy fidget toys, flap his hands and pace, regrouping for the next class of intensive interactions with people.

Unfortunately, that's where he was found by two of the most powerful kids in school. Because he had chosen an out-of-the-way spot, no adults could see it happening. The bullies started out by just teasing him a bit. Then they took his fidget toys, played tricks on him and taught him to say offensive words to girls. Trying to get away, he switched his location to an alcove on the other side of the building, but his classmates predatorily came looking for Nathan. Word got around and the crowds grew to watch the "show." Taking his belongings and making him cry, exerting their power, Darlene and Renee flirted one minute and taunted the next. For days, the girls subtly followed Nathan inside the school and out, quietly goading him and leading him on.

As the girls got brasher, a teacher's assistant noticed, immediately reported the bullying and the school's protocol was activated. Thankfully, the administration had already set up a system which included dealing with the bullies, the onlookers who didn't report the bullying, the target—Nathan—and the school staff.

Long-term effects

One of the most painful difficulties for people with autism/ Asperger's who are bullied is reliving the bullying event over and over. I've worked with adults who describe being bullied many years earlier as if it happened today, bringing all of the emotions and trauma with it. "Their main way of trying to understand why they were singled out is to repeatedly replay the events in their thoughts. The person is reliving, but *not resolving* past injustices. This can be a daily experience even though the incidents occurred decades earlier" (Attwood 2007, p.102, italics mine). In my counseling work with people on the autism spectrum, assessing for trauma symptoms is a regular part of my treatment intake process. Almost without exception, ASD clients (see "Autism-ese" Glossary) aged 12 and older will have experienced some kind of unresolved, bullying trauma.

Sleuthing out evidence

As a parent how can you tell if your child is being bullied? The list below can get you started on your search for evidence:

- A change in the way your child interacts with family or friends. For example: more sullen and withdrawn, more agitated or perhaps even violent.

- Pleading with you to drive him/her to or from school.

- Changing her/his usual route for walking to or from school.

- Peculiar loss of property or personal items, including money.

- Uncharacteristic hunger when getting home from school could indicate a bully is stealing your child's lunch or lunch money.

- Unexplained bruising, scrapes or cuts.

- A change in the way your child expresses anger.

- Your child using "bullying language" with siblings or other kids.

- Depression symptoms like loss of appetite, a drop in grades, expressions of not wanting to live. Attwood (2007) reports for some children suicide is "perceived as the only way to stop the emotional pain that bullying is causing in the child's daily life" (p.100). I encourage parents to take these statements seriously. If your child is in this much emotional pain, seek counseling for him/her.

- Your child responding "with violence in an attempt to deter the bullying" (Attwood 2007, p.101).

- "A change in special interests, from relatively benign topics, such as vehicles and insects, to an interest in weapons, the martial arts and violent films, especially films with a theme of retribution. The child's drawings may also express violence, retaliation and retribution" (Attwood 2007, p.101).

Be their voice

Many of our children with autism/Asperger's don't have the verbal or emotional expressive skills to communicate what is happening to them when adults aren't around. As parents, we can harness our own fear of bullying by looking for clues, asking questions and acting on the evidence. The possibility of bullying is very real at school, in public and even at home. We have the distinct privilege and responsibility to be the voice of our children who have a tough time speaking up for themselves.

On a lighter note

In her book *Autism: Living with my brother Tiger*, my friend Linda Lee writes of her neurotypical son Jason's perspective of dealing with a bully: "One day last year an older boy was trying to bully me. I told my parents and they asked me what did I do. I answered, 'I didn't say or do anything, but I thought to myself that he shouldn't mess with a second grader who knew long division'" (Lee 2006, p.36).

Coach yourself through Bullying

1. What meaning does the word "bullying" carry for you?

2. How can this meaning help or hinder you in being your child's "voice"?

3. What changes in behavior have you observed? Write them down, because you may need to communicate these observations to someone else.

4. What clues do you notice which might indicate your child is being bullied? If needed, refer back to the section Sleuthing out evidence. Write them down.

5. What does the evidence point to? Write it down.

6. If needed, where can you access more resources on bullying? *Example:* Tony Attwood's book, searching the internet, calling your child's school or school district, a local counselor with ASD experience and understanding, a coach who specializes in ASD, etc.

7. What conversations need to happen? With whom? How soon?

8. What is your desired outcome with each conversation?

9. What will you do?

10. When will you do it? Date: _____ Time: _____

11. How will you know when you have accomplished your desired outcome(s)?

12. If bullying is a factor in your child's life, how will you nurture him/her through this difficulty?

Ideas to take away with you

What's your "take-away" from coaching yourself through Bullying? Writing it down anchors the learning.

11
Stuck Spots

You can't get there from here! Stuck. Entrenched. Arrrrgh! I despise that feeling. Many parents of children with autism experience it regularly: stuck spots in the cycles of life that hold us hostage with no visible means of change. Perhaps the concern is school placement, lack of respite services, financial constraints, daycare, safety, or sleeping. What is it for you? You know—the perpetual concern that gets your gut grinding, your pulse racing and your anxiety pumping?

For 13 years, the phrase that made my blood run cold was, "summer vacation." Even with Extended School Year (usually two to three days a week for four weeks), a structured home schedule, hired skill-trainers and a village of supportive friends, my boy would still regress considerably. By August, he and I were wrung out like dish rags with multiple meltdowns, intense parenting and lots of tears on both sides.

Several years ago, I went back to school to earn my Masters in Counseling with a view to working with families impacted by autism. The classes were great and I loved the clinical work, but a slice of the pie was missing. Not all autism families need counseling. Many parents need someone to come alongside and hold a space for *them* to sort and decide on next steps. That's when I learned about coaching—the missing piece of the pie.

In June of 2005, while in the throes of my last year of grad school, I signed up for four intensive coaching classes. The instructors asked for someone to be coached in front of the class, someone with a stuck spot, with a dogging dilemma. Wow, did I have one! I immediately volunteered.

Clustered around a table, five of my classmates were instructed to "seamlessly" coach me—meaning they would take turns asking coaching questions around my stuckness. On my team of coaches were two dear friends who for years had tracked with my summer-marathon exhaustion. A camera focused down on me for the convenience of future classes.

I told my story of having tried everything, of my growing anxiety over the summer stretching out before me, and of my utter fear of the looming fatigue in August. Every summer had been the same; there was no hope this would be any different. Tears flowed. Darn camera.

The coaching team sat in shock. My two close friends lowered their heads, as stuck as I was. How many hours over how many years had we gone round and round this same subject? Then un-coaching questions peppered me. The others were trying their best, but suggestions weren't helpful—believe me I had tried everything from accessing support in my faith community, to county resources, to a variety of conventional-to-ridiculous interventions. We autism-impacted families attempt anything and everything!

With tears coursing down my face, I kept repeating, "This is not helpful… This is not helpful." Finally, the ten minutes was over, much to the relief of everyone in the room.

Moments later in the ladies room, I leaned over the sink, splashed my face with cold water, looked in the mirror and asked myself, "What in the world just happened?"

But, you know, something shifted. Even though the coaching was, well…uh…terrible, something happened to me internally, although I wasn't aware of it immediately. That summer while being coached weekly, I decreased my work days from four to three. At home, I started my own coaching business and Cope to Hope was born! I wrote a business plan, developed a website, made contacts with over 100 people and started writing articles. By the end of summer, Jordan and I were still worn out, but not quite as brutally. Everything was not magically fixed, but we were on a different track.

Since then, our summers have been progressively more successful. My work schedule is now flexible. I plan for "Autism in August," knowing that we can't do many extra activities. I still make judgment errors, like volunteering Jordan and me to help move the Chamber of Commerce office. In August? What was I thinking?! We keep a quiet, steady routine with a minimal number of extras. My community of friends know that our availability is limited, saying "Oh, yeah, it's August!"

What did I learn? Trust the coaching process. It really does work.

Coach yourself through Stuck Spots

Try to complete this exercise in one sitting, approximately 20 minutes.

1. Where you're sitting right now, bring a stuck spot to the front of your mind. Got it? Feel the frustration of it, the yuckiness of the stuckness. *Eeew, what kind of exercise is this anyway?* Now, give this stuck spot a name—one or two words.

   Name of Perspective #1_____

   _____

2. Get up, move to a different location in the room. For this exercise to be most helpful, getting up and moving is essential. Look back at Perspective #1. What do you notice? For example: *what does your body language tell you? Were you hunched over with a clenched jaw?*

   What do you notice about this new place?

   What has changed?

   What has stayed the same?

   Now, give this spot a name—one or two words.

   Name of Perspective #2 _____

   _____

3. Get up again and move to a different location where you can look outside.

   What do you see from this vantage point?

   How does looking outside change your perspective?

   What is your body telling you now?

Look back at Perspective #2. What do you notice?

Now, give this spot a name—one or two words.

Name of Perspective #3 _____

_____

4. Last time, get up and move again to a different location and imagine some wild, goofy or bizarre perspective. *Examples*: "The Parakeet Perspective" or the "Sky-diving Perspective"—just be sure it's "out there."

   A side note from Ruth: When I did this exercise with my own coach, I couldn't think of a weird example. He threw out, "How about the Harley-Davidson Perspective?" At first, I couldn't think of anything, but started to picture myself climbing on a "hog," revving the engine, and taking off. This was definitely the perspective I wanted to keep as a metaphor for my life. "Get on your Harley and ride" is a phrase I recall whenever I'm starting a new adventure in my professional and personal life. In fact I often wear my Harley-Davidson socks when teaching coach trainings!

   Name of Perspective #4 _____

   _____

   What does this new perspective give you?

   What does it take away?

   Look back at Perspective #3, what do you notice?

   What has changed in this perspective?

5. List all four perspectives:

   Perspective #1 _____

Perspective #2 _____

Perspective #3 _____

Perspective #4 _____

Which one do you want to stay in today?

How will you remind yourself to revisit this perspective?

Which one do you not want to go back to?

How will you notice when you've slipped back to it?

6. What have you learned about your stuck spot?

7. Write down the first thing that pops into your mind when asked the following question:

    What is one thing you can do differently?

    Even a small change can start loosening the stuck spot. Please don't discount the first idea.

8. What will you do?

    When will you do it? Date: _____ Time: _____

Ideas to take away with you

What's your "take-away" from coaching yourself through Stuck Spots? Writing it down anchors the learning.

SECTION II:

PARENTING NEUROTYPICAL SIBLINGS

12

Asymmetrical Development

◇◇◇◇◇◇◇◇◇◇◇◇◇◇◇◇◇◇◇◇◇◇◇◇◇◇◇◇◇◇◇◇◇◇◇◇◇◇

All kids are different, that's for sure. But if you have at least one on the autism spectrum and at least one NT (see "Autism-ese" Glossary), then you have a challenge. You're raising two or more children developing at radically different rates. How to accommodate that at home?

Three different families

The Reed family's oldest son was severely impacted by autism with delays in every area. The next child, an NT daughter passed him up developmentally at about 24 months. Unexpectedly, she was the "older" sister, even though she was four years younger. How does a family parent through that?

The Willford's first daughter Flohra was precociously neurotypical. Boy and girl twins born five years later were diagnosed with PDD.NOS (Pervasive Developmental Disorder. Not Otherwise Specified) at 24 months, and classic autism at age three. Flohra was thrown into a caregiver role with her younger siblings and by age nine related to them more as a therapist than as a sister. Because of her abilities, additional adult-like responsibilities were assigned and she grew up miss-ing out on some fun that comes from just being a naïve kid. Mom and Dad's hands were full with her younger siblings, resulting in Flohra's typical developmental needs coming in at a distant third.

The Castilians were busy parents with five stair-stepchil-dren—boy/girl/girl/boy/girl—all roughly two years apart. The family recognized their middle daughter Kelsey was quirky because of her atypical use of language, her intense interest in squirrels, and her insistence on eating only white foods. Her parents, however, were shocked when the school diagnosed her with Asperger's at the age of ten. Mounds of reading helped them recognize the pattern of relating that had developed be-tween their five children. The older siblings watched out for bullies seeking to torment Kelsey but also got mad when she just didn't "get" the subtle rules of a new game. The younger siblings learned to communicate with her by reading *Amelia Bedelia* (Parish 1976) but got angry when her obsessive routines got in the way of their plans.

In their book *What About Me?* Siegel and Silverstein (1994) write compassionately to parents:

> It is easy to minimize the concerns of a small child. To do otherwise requires that extra effort of *stepping into the child's world*. This is a difficult task even under near-perfect conditions, one of the reasons child-rearing is such a hard job. Add the burden of raising an autis-tic child, with his or her unpredictable outbursts and demands, and there is very little patience left over for the effective parenting of the rest of the children (p.13, italics mine).

In homes with any age of special needs children, in the process of just surviving, parents can get sidetracked from the focus of parenting *all* the children in the home. Strength to you, on this journey.

Coach yourself through Asymmetrical Development

1. Who are the people at your house? Draw your family as shown in the example below.

Example

Dad		Mom		
Trevor		Molly		Max
Age 12		Age 8		Age 6
Dev. age 4		Dev. age 8		Dev. age 6

2. Answer the following set of questions for each child, starting with the developmentally oldest first. Keep in mind that IQ is very different from developmental and social abilities:

Name_____

- What extra responsibilities does this child carry because of having a sibling on spectrum?

- What extra privileges does this child receive for the extra responsibilities?

- What responsibilities is this child carrying that she/he shouldn't be?

- How will you respectfully relieve them of that responsibility?

- What's missing in this child's life that could add richness, joy or happiness to his/her experience growing up?

- ○ On a scale of 1–10, how accessible would this child say you are as a parent? 1 = not accessible at all. 10 = absolutely accessible.

- ○ What would it take to increase that score by 0.5?

- ○ What is one thing you will do this week to add richness, joy or happiness to this child's life?

3. After you have answered the above questions for *each child* in your home, narrow down your own action point:

4. What is one thing you will do?

5. When will you do it?

   Date: _____ Time: _____

6. How committed are you to doing it? (Example: 90%, 40%, etc.)

7. What is one "speed bump" you could anticipate getting in your way?

8. What's your plan for getting over the speed bump?

9. How will you know when you're done with this particular action?

10. How will you celebrate?

Ideas to take away with you

What's your "take-away" from coaching yourself through Asymmetrical Development? Writing it down anchors the learning.

13

Autism-free Zones

◇◇◇◇◇◇◇◇◇◇◇◇

In public, we're a spectacle. Clerks in stores remember us. I'm the red-headed mom with the red-headed kids, one of whom is 6 foot 4 inches and severely impacted by autism. Don't get me wrong, I'm not ashamed, not one bit. I'm proud of my kids and hold my head high. We just make, let's say, a *lasting impression.*

Jordan's "dkadeee" gets louder and higher pitched the happier he is. You can imagine the shrieks of delight emanating from the toy aisle! To manage the sensory input of people, fluorescent lights and background music, he flaps and stims ("autism-ese" jargon for self-stimulation)—sometimes a little, sometimes a lot. Enjoying being together, he and I often run through some of our favorite dialogues from classic children's movies, laughing at the jokes that have been funny to us for 15 plus years. *That's such a great thing about autism at our house; the same joke is funny every time!*

When Jordan was younger, the staring, the raised eyebrows, the perceived disapproval were daggers in my gut. For years, I carried cards that could be handed to people stating something like, "Please don't let my child's behavior alarm you. My child has autism." On the back was some educational information about autism. Not sure I ever actually gave one of those away, but it was nice knowing I had them.

With my daughter Gracey being the youngest in our family, she has never known anything different. Jordan is Jordan. But around her 5th grade year, his public behavior started causing a measure of embarrassment. And who could blame her? At times, I do still get embarrassed and I'm his mom! *Can I really admit that? Yeah, I think I need to.* Strange isn't it that I can feel proud of him and a bit embarrassed all at the same time? Through the years, as I've grown up, I've become more comfortable with this type of internal ambivalence.

Taking a break from autism

Enter autism-free zones. Sometimes siblings need normal. Dinner in a sit-down restaurant, a trip to the clothing store or hot chocolate at a local coffee shop can be a refreshing break from the weight of being the sister or brother of an autism-impacted child. A couple of years ago, my daughter and I took off for a weekend of wild shopping at a "supermall" about three hours away. We laughed till we cried in a restaurant. A spectacle? Yes, but not because of autism. She saw a cockroach walking along the windowsill. We told the manager and suddenly they gave us all kinds of free food. We got the giggles and couldn't stop laughing.

I fell asleep propped up against a three-way mirror, waiting while she tried on a mountain of clothes. The most poignant moment was walking into Wal-Mart as a family quickly exited with an obviously autistic child in tow. Poor guy, he was melting down and terribly distraught. I said a prayer for the family under my breath, but Gracey and I just kept walking. This time, this day, the public meltdown didn't include us. She wasn't the horrified sibling trying to dissolve into the woodwork.

Obviously, no sibling can be autism-free 24 hours a day. Providing autism-free zones doesn't mean we indulge our neurotypical children. But, autism-free zones do communicate:

- "I see you."

- "I appreciate that you need normal sometimes."

- "You are just as important in this family as anybody."

- "You've got a difficult job, and I want to give you a little respite."

Autism-free zones show respect, care and kindness. And a most important message—*every* child in this family is valued.

Coach yourself through Autism-free Zones

1. Which of your children is most in need of an autism-free zone?

2. What are his/her particular interests?

3. What does that child like to do? List at least eight things.

4. Who might she/he like to invite along?

5. When are you going to do it?

   Day: _____ Time: _____

6. Knowing you, what could get in your way of making this happen?

7. Who can you ask to hold you accountable to do this thing that you want to do?

Ideas to take away with you

What's your "take-away" from coaching yourself through Autism-free Zones? Writing it down anchors the learning.

14

Parenting Your Child's Strengths (Neurotypical Children)

When my daughter was born, I held the darling, little red-headed sweetie in my arms letting the gravity of parenting sink in. I'm the mom.

> As parents, it's important for us to be our children's advocates—the people in their lives who help them see and focus on the best in them. There will always be plenty of people around our children who see their weaknesses and label their behaviors in less-than-positive ways. As a parent, you can be one of the people in your child's life who helps him or her see life from a strengths perspective. (Gallup Organization 2007, p.3)

True non-strength confession

I am not athletic. I like to work-out at the gym, but I'm really bad at sports. Believe me I'm not overstating my inability.

In 8th grade, I was the tallest player on the basketball team and scored two points the entire season. In the same game, I scored two points for the opposing team. Many memories flood my brain of standing at home plate in a "friendly" softball game with infielders shouting "easy out!" And they were right. The one time I hit a home run, I was four months pregnant. Looking back, I realize the other team was coddling the expectant mother "running" around the bases.

In my senior year of high school, the basketball coach coaxed and pleaded for me to go out for the team. After all, at that time, I was 5 foot 10 inches. I envisioned the Haxtun (Colorado) Fightin' Bulldogs winning game after game with me as their center. Before try-outs, wisdom won out in a frank conversation with myself, "Ruth, this is your senior year. Do you *really* want to play a sport you're not good at? What activities would you have to remove from your life to play basketball? What do you enjoy? What are you good at?" Thankfully, I decided instead to throw myself into Choir, Drama, and Future Business Leaders of America (FBLA). Much as I hated to admit it at the time, I have limitations.

The reality is that a person who has always struggled with numbers is unlikely to be a great accountant or statistician. And the person without much natural empathy will never be able to comfort an agitated customer in the warm and sincere way that the great empathizers can. "Even the legendary Michael Jordan, who embodied the power of raw talent on a basketball court, could not become, well, the Michael Jordan of golf or baseball, no matter how hard he tried" (Rath 2007, p.7).

All these years later, I'm happy with my high school decision. Music remains an extremely important part of my life and I serve on my church worship team. I've started two businesses. The drama background has paid off many times parenting my son with autism. He has worked patiently with me to learn my lines from dozens of movie dialogues, which we now "perform" together at random times—in the car, on a hiking trail, while grocery shopping—much to our own amusement and no one else's.

Strength-based research

After 40 years of research studying the talents of individuals, The Gallup Organization discovered a simple principle: "Successful people understand their talents, and build their lives upon them" (Gallup Organization 2007). Since many of us adults function best when utilizing our talents, how can we parent with the same mindset?

The neurotypical siblings in your home are developing unique strengths. No one in the world has the same mix of aptitudes. Living with a brother or sister with autism will shape them. Thankfully, tools are available to help them increase their strengths.

You might check out the online strength-discovery instrument for students called *The Clifton Youth StrengthsExplorer* (Gallup Organization 2007). The process includes a 10 to 14-year-old taking a fun online assessment with an immediate printable report of his or her top three themes. Workbooks for youth and parents include coaching exercises to make the most of a student's strengths. Many parents—including me—are in the habit of focusing on our children's weaknesses and trying to shore them up. Don't get me wrong, children do need guidance and correcting. And our words can carry unimaginable influence. "We are not always aware of the language we use and the weakening effects it can and does have on children. They hear everything we say and absorb it even when it is not directed at them" (Fox 2008, p.24).

Jenifer Fox's excellent resource is entitled *Your Child's Strengths: Discover Them, Develop Them, Use Them* (2008). She discusses "The Weakness Habit," "A Strengths Awakening," and includes a practical section with over 90 pages featuring the *Create Your Future, Play to Your Strengths Workbook*. In it, she reminds parents that:

> Things seldom turn out as planned. We cannot simply prepare our children for lives of security; we must also instill in them a sense of hope and the ability to be *resilient* in the face of uncertainty... The discovery and development of inner strengths will help shape children's understanding of what *moves them forward with purpose,* as well as teach them how to cope with uncertain times (Fox 2008, p.164, italics mine).

When picturing my children as adults, I like that word *resilient*, defined as "springing back; rebounding" and "recovering readily from illness, depression, adversity, or the like; buoyant." (Random House 2008). When times get tough, it's their talents and strengths that will bring momentum to their lives. We parents have an amazing opportunity to fan the flame of our children's strengths, to give them a solid foundation which can instill an ability to be resilient. Many neurotypical siblings are well on their way. They're learning to be flexible and to negotiate while practicing compassion and kindness. Imagine what every member of your family could gain by living from strengths!

Coach yourself through Parenting Your Child's Strengths (Neurotypical Children)

1. What do you observe about your child's strengths? Including the following: (Try not to assign meaning, just notice)

   a. likes/dislikes

   b. things he/she likes to do

   c. inclinations, bents, tendencies

   d. idiosyncrasies/quirks

   e. personality traits.

2. What accomplishments has your child enjoyed?

3. How can you help build on the accomplishments your child has had?

4. How can you help create more?

5. What does it mean to develop parenting strategies with _____ the adult in mind? Fill in your son or daughter's name. *Example*: Caitlyn the adult.

6. How helpful would a strengths assessment tool be for your child? For you as the parent?

7. What's your next step?

8. What will you do?

9. When will you do it? Date: _____ Time: _____

10. Who will you ask to make sure you do it?

Ideas to take away with you

What's your "take-away" from coaching yourself through Parenting Your Child's Strengths (Neurotypical Children). Writing it down anchors the learning.

15

Fairness

<<<<<<<<<<<<<<<<<<<<<<<<<>

"Life is not fair."

That statement irritates me. The statement is true. But it still irritates me. For families with a mix of siblings—neurotypical and ASD the battle cry, "That's not fair!" is commonly heard. When the needs of children in the same home vary drastically, the dilemma can be constant. For most parents, the automatic reflex is to square off by matching the intensity of the battle cry with one of their own. What might it be like for a typical sibling if the parent took more of a "shoulder to shoulder" stance, and tried to hear the need behind what could be a very annoying comment?

One family's story

The Ericksons have a unique approach to fairness between siblings. The mom Diana reports confidently, "We haven't 'done' fair. We have done what each kid needed."

An active family of four they live in a quaint mountain town where Dale farms Christmas trees. When preschool son Jack was diagnosed with autism in the medium to high range of functioning, it was difficult for everyone. Diana immediately engaged services for occupational therapy, speech therapy and early intervention. Three years older than her brother, daughter Haley was already well-established and thriving in her small-town life and school. They loved their rural lifestyle.

With strength in her voice, Diana tells the story of their decision: the family would "do what's best for everybody" including Jack *and* Haley. "We were never willing to move" or "turn our lives upside down." Making Jack the center of the family wasn't good for anyone. Dave and Diana made choices with *all* family members in mind. They "didn't have to break the bank, looking for the silver bullet" to cure Jack's autism.

Living on a mountain, the Ericksons enjoy hiking. Every Sunday, regardless of his attitude, Jack came along on the family hike. The parents decided, "We are going to be normal and do our usual thing" and they "had to live through a lot of temper tantrums." Sometimes, when Jack protested loudly, he was told, "We're a family and this is what the family is doing." Calling themselves the "loud family," they still chuckle about never seeing wildlife on their many hikes.

The decision paid off. Over the years Jack (now 12) learned *he* was a part of the family. Now his middle school teachers comment on how "well-adjusted" he is and willing to try new things. Last summer at camp he introduced himself to his cabinmates: "Hi, I'm Jack and I have autism," and went on to a positive week with a group of guys he hadn't known before. Of course, there was plenty of anxious nail-biting for Mom who greatly wanted him to experience success.

In earlier times, some family activities would not work for all four of them to attend, like going to plays and movies. Theaters were impossible for Jack to tolerate because of the noise and intensity of sensory input. So, Diana, Dale and Haley would go to a movie by themselves and leave Jack with a babysitter.

Through the years, Diana and Dale worked hard to help him tolerate seeing a film, by having him wear both earplugs, then one earplug, and giving the option to excuse himself and leave the room for a few minutes if he was overloading.

Eventually this allowed them to include the whole family in a fun trip to the movies, which fit with their values of doing things together as a foursome. Jack now reflects on those days saying, "It was so loud and I never knew what to expect...but now I know unexpected things happen in movies." Diana looks back remembering, "We tried a lot of things so he could be as much a part of the family as possible."

Since his kids were little, Dale has intentionally taken them individually out to restaurants, hiking and backpacking for one-on-one time. At first, Jack protested, but now backpacking with Dad is a highlight of the summer.

What works for this family? Diana emphasizes this is *one* family. What works for them might not work for you—and that is totally OK:

- Try pushing your child out of his/her comfort zone occasionally to see what happens. Doing so can be a good stretch for the autism-impact child and a message of fairness to typical siblings.

- If an intervention doesn't work, reintroduce it weeks or months later, because, "As kids mature, they change."

- Even some kids with autism find ways to manipulate you. One sibling I know is very astute at discerning when her brother is "faking it." Be open to the influence of the opinions and experiences of your typical kids.

- Keeping a paper and pen in the car to write out a quick stick-figure picture schedule can prevent meltdowns. (See "Autism-ese" Glossary and Chapter 1: Meltdowns.)

Many times a child will protest because of not knowing what's happening next. Little pictures can give a simple and soothing explanation.

- Rewards work!

- Using the phrase "First _____, then_____". Example: "*First* hiking, *then* out to dinner." Starting with the unwanted task and end with some kind of reward sometimes prevents hours of discord.

- If the family plan goes awry and the child doesn't get the anticipated reward, make sure to reward him/her some other way that day. Example: increasing computer time by 30 minutes when you get home.

- Life isn't about "fairness":

  ○ Jack received things Haley did not.

  ○ Haley received things Jack did not.

- As much as she can, Diana tries to give her time equally to each child.

- Sixteen-year old, Haley is much more aware of the "fairness" issue and on occasion will say, "You love Jack more." Wisely, Diana doesn't get angry and protest at the inaccurate statement. She moves toward her daughter, quietly saying, "I can see why you would feel that way." Frankly, Mom does have to put more effort and attention into parenting Jack. The statement, however, informs Mom that her daughter needs more one-on-one time, even if it's small.

- Set boundaries for the safety and comfort of each child. Examples:

- To the child with autism, "Knock on your sister's door before entering."

- To the neurotypical sibling, "Speak to your brother with respect."

- Pick your battles! Don't expect compliance on every issue. Choose carefully.

- Use what works with your child.

No, life isn't fair. Some people have greater challenges to overcome. *Don't we families with autism/Asperger's know it?* Life can, however, have great meaning, purpose and even enjoyment for parents and kids.

Diana reflects back on their early parenting choices of expecting participation and rewarding. She sees it as a rhythm for Jack's life. He is open to new experiences because:

"What *we* did, *he* did."

Coach yourself through Fairness

1. Which of your children is talking about "fairness?"

2. What's your guess about what she/he needs?

3. How can you check out the accuracy of your guess?

4. What will you do to help meet the need?

5. When will you do it? Date: _____ Time: _____

6. How will you know when the need is met?

7. What does this need tell you about your child?

Ideas to take away with you

What's your "take-away" from coaching yourself through Fairness? Writing it down anchors the learning.

16

Message from a Grown Sibling

◇◇◇◇◇◇◇◇◇◇◇◇◇◇◇◇◇◇◇◇◇◇◇◇◇◇◇◇◇◇◇◇◇◇◇◇◇◇◇

Leah had autism at her house before autism was cool. Well, maybe not *cool*, but before it was widely known.

Her older brother Jim was born in 1978 and she came along four years later. Still in the throes of the "Refrigerator Mother" era (see "Autism-ese" Glossary), Leah's mom was determined that her little girl would be the child in the family who talked and read, proving Jim's autism was not Mom's fault. Her mom was right, it wasn't her fault, yet young Leah still felt pressure to perform.

Leah's fun early memories include grabbing onto the back of big brother's jeans and being dragged around the house. Even in preschool, Leah figured out that Jim "wasn't normal." He was in a different class at school and they walked to his room to pick him up. Most people didn't do that. The kids in his group were dissimilar to other kids, and the sharp four-year-old noticed this. Jim was different, no big deal.

"I never felt young." Leah recalls being treated as if she was older and that she liked it. Her job in the family was to be a helper to her parents and they sure needed her. Jim was a handful and Leah, the smart, cooperative girl, took on her role with vigor. She loved it! Four years later when her twin sisters were born, her responsibilities tripled. Leah's attention from Mom and Dad came last. That's just the way it was.

Once a year, Leah would go on a weekend away with Mom or Dad—fun memories of backpacking, amusement parks and ski trips. During these years, with the tasks at home, she couldn't really have friends over. On the rare occasions she did have her own company, it was "a huge production," with a week of house cleaning and preparation. The result was only casual contact at school and few close connections with friends.

Leah's parents were co-chairs of Montana's Autism Association (MAA), so their family telephone rang off the hook with people in crisis. Autism resources were scarce and anyone with more expertise was utilized as a tutor. Having listened to her parents walk people through typical autism emergencies, Leah started fielding calls herself, helping people and giving suggestions. Even as young as age nine, she was genuinely helpful as she learned from watching many families at MAA picnics and from living with her own family. (In retrospect, she says, "Now, that seems quite developmentally inappropriate.") A large part of her identity was about taking care of things and knowing about autism.

At that stage, Leah took pride in her "perfect" family. Their motto was, "We do hard things and we're good at it." She reports this family slogan getting her through to her teens, when her family became distasteful to her. That's when Jim started irritating her. He was older, becoming "more aggressive, misbehaving and annoying." She still could influence him in ways no one else could, so sometimes calming his meltdowns was her assignment, which definitely added to her stress.

Teenage Leah wanted her own space and wished her life included something more. Thankfully, Dad noticed her need and made arrangements with the across-the-road neighbor for riding lessons. Horses were Leah's passion. She worked at the stable, paid for half of her lessons and got her own horse at age 17. This was *her* world which had nothing to do with autism or helping her parents. And it was extremely important. Horses got her through adolescence.

Now as an adult woman in grad school, Leah reflects on the blessings she received from growing up with a brother with autism. Leah sees herself as compassionate. She's studying to be a counselor after all. She possesses a deep understanding that not everybody is the same. She has great "compassion for the underdog and people who have hard things in their lives." Leah appreciates the "club" of autism—the knowingness that happens when people with autism in their lives connect with each other.

Leah's message to parents? It is widely used banking analogy that parents hold an "emotional bank account" with each child. Families' lives often revolve around autism, requiring frequent "withdrawals" to be taken out of the siblings' "accounts" just to keep the autism/Asperger's member afloat. Leah recommends parents make frequent "deposits" into the accounts of siblings. In her case, "It would have helped to be acknowledged for what I did more than once a year." In adolescence, Leah's horses somehow filled in some of the deficits in her account. "If I hadn't had the horses, it would have been really hard."

Examples of withdrawals she remembers were events like her winning a basketball at a fast-food restaurant and being asked to give it to Jim because he really liked it. Of course, her dad promised to get her something else to replace it, but asked her to give the basketball up by saying, "Look what Jim has to deal with." But she really wanted that ball and it *was* hers. On some occasions, why couldn't he be the one to not get what he wanted? Why couldn't they tell him "no" and just weather the meltdown? And speaking of meltdowns, if he is allowed to fall apart emotionally, why can't I sometimes?

Before we start pointing the finger at Leah's parents, saying "How could they?" let's remember some of the desperate moments we as parents have encountered and the huge sacrifices we've asked of the typical siblings in our own homes. (For more on this topic, see Chapter 15: Fairness.)

As a sibling, Leah's message is for parents to regularly talk to their other kids, saying, "This is really hard for you. You're dealing with a lot, and I'm really proud of you." It doesn't take much to encourage a sibling.

Yes, parents are often overwhelmed with the sheer magnitude of parenting a child with autism/Asperger's and siblings are faced with an *equally massive* challenge. Emotional deposits can be as simple as saying "You've been given a tough job and you're amazing at it!"

Leah's final words to parents in her own voice are:

- "Invest in each sibling as much as you invest in the autistic kid."

- "Be willing to talk to siblings and validate their experience."

- "The sibling's identity is to be a part of that family. Autism isn't just the parents' problem; it's also the sibling's problem."

- "Don't be afraid to process with your other kids about their autism challenges—it's going to take a whole lot more processing than in 'normal' families."

Leah's compassion and empathy is readily evident even at first meeting. The challenge of growing up in an autism-impacted family has forged character and perception beyond her years.

Will she be an excellent counselor? Oh, yeah. Her compassion comes from first-hand experience with tenacity *and* pain *and* hope. And her unique perspective? She is a champion of underdogs.

Coach yourself through Parenting Siblings

"Accounts" Ledger

	Child's name	Child's name	Child's name	Child's name
Current "balance"	————	————	————	————
A recent significant "deposit"	+	+	+	+
What your child would count as a recent significant "deposit"	+	+	+	+
A recent significant "withdrawal"	–	–	–	–
What your child would count as a recent significant "withdrawal"	–	–	–	–
Adjusted "balance"				

1. Fill out the "Accounts Ledger" above.

2. What future "withdrawals" do you anticipate? Consider this question for each child.

3. What "deposits" will you make in each account?

4. What small deposits can you make? Even pennies make a difference over time.

5. Which sibling seems to have the lowest current balance?

6. What "deposit" will you make specifically for that child this week? Today?

    Date: _____ Time: _____

7. How can you make that "deposit" bigger?

8. What could get in your way of making this deposit?

For further study on the topic of siblings of all ages, an excellent resource is the book *What About Me?* (Siegel and Silverstein 1994).

Ideas to take away with you

What's your "takeaway" from coaching yourself through Parenting Siblings? Writing it down anchors the learning.

SECTION III:

PARENT CARE AND LONG-TERM HEALTH

17

Comparison

◇◇◇◇◇◇◇◇◇◇◇◇◇◇◇◇◇◇◇◇◇◇◇◇◇◇

You're a parent.

I'm a parent.

Your child is a unique individual.

My child is a unique individual.

If only we could leave it at that.

If we're truthful, most of us occasionally put pressure on others to parent the way we do it. With so many unknowns about ASD, perhaps, somehow, it validates our choices in this uncertain maze. Incidentally, my hope for this book is not to be a "voice" of pressure, but rather a "voice" of hope.

Many of us parents play the comparison game with each other and, worse yet, with our children. Almost always, the game is unproductive and positions us as rivals rather than allies. What can happen when we decide not to assess ourselves against each other?

A freeing friendship

Thanks to autism, Dena and I have been friends for over ten years. We're very different. She's 5 foot 2 inches. I'm 5 foot 9 inches. She lives in the country. I live in a neighborhood. She does triathlons. I do yoga.

Busy with family, our contact is intermittent, sometimes going months in between. But there's a refreshing knowingness between us. We've shared phone calls, resources, car conversations, a kids' swimming instructor, funny stories and coffee, always gaining strength and ideas from each other. Our friendship has provided safety to confide our experiences as moms of boys with autism, including our doubts, our mistakes and our treatment choices. In this friendship, "comparison" is a tool for encouragement.

Our sons are very different people. Her son is a lean, wiry middle schooler. My son is a strapping, wide-shouldered high schooler. Both are loving and humorous. Her son has an aid in an inclusive classroom and is doing pretty well academically. My son, in addition to autism is severely impacted by learning disabilities. Thankfully, the discrepancy in their skill levels hasn't made us opposed to one another. We're still allies.

Around 1999, Dena and I lightheartedly confessed we were saying "no" to watching most of the TV news magazines' features on autism because, at that time, nearly all had a predictable story line with a fairy-tale ending:

1. Doctors diagnose the child with little prospect for improvement.

2. Mom works tirelessly doing some type of therapy with her child.

3. Astonishingly, the child ends up not having autism in the end.

4. Throughout the narrative lies the insinuation that if every mom worked this hard with her child, the autism would go away.

Plain and simple, the feature stories were too painful to watch. We were glad for the families with such miracle results while being extremely sad over our own normalcy. Predictably afterwards, well-meaning people clamored to tell us the latest scoop, saying "I saw this show on TV and immediately thought of you." Very sweet of them, but how do you explain that you didn't watch it? Or even worse that you have already tried the treatment and it didn't work with your child? Separately, Dena and I had come to like conclusions.

Reality list (Isbell 2008)

To like conclusions resulting in a list of bedrock truths we come back to when unknowing people make uninformed comments.

1. I work just as tirelessly with my son. In fact, he is really lucky and blessed to have me as his mom.

2. I know him better than anyone and I trust my intuition about what he needs.

3. He's making progress but not astonishingly so.

4. He's doing the best he could possibly be doing.

5. He's a terrific kid with endearing characteristics.

6. He still definitely has autism.

7. Some children do make pronounced gains—*yea! I celebrate with them and their families!*

8. My son hasn't made the same astounding leaps in progress. That hurts.

9. Even if a mom pours out her very soul for her child (as most moms do), some children just make slow gains.

10. A life with autism isn't a competition between moms for an award of "who does the most."

11. Autism treatment is not one-size-fits-all. The suggestions given to us by our multi-disciplinary treatment teams are a *menu* rather than a *to-do list*. We pick and choose what works for *our* child.

Dena and I still run into each other. We brainstorm, respect each other's wisdom and sometimes borrow strength to go against conventional flow. Now that we're 10 and 15 years into this journey, we have more confidence in our own abilities to make decisions, to advocate for our sons and to say "no" when needed.

Comparison can be helpful, like when Dena and I compare experiences and validate each other. Comparison can also be toxic and discouraging, like when I watch the extraordinary news magazine stories and end up feeling like a completely ineffective parent afterward.

It helps to go back to my Reality List and remember what is true. It also helps to spend time with supportive people (not those who *should* be supportive, but those who really *are* supportive).

Come to think of it, I'm ready to have coffee again. How 'bout it, Dena?

Coach yourself through Comparison

1. What good decisions have you made as a parent? Write your own Reality List.

2. What have you learned from your mistakes?

3. In what area(s) are you comparing yourself to other parents? What is the result? What do you start telling yourself after comparing? We'll call this My Words to Me.

4. Run your Words to Me through the ROLF test (Martindale 2008b):

    a. **R**eal—are your words based in reality or made up? *Example*: non-real words: "Her son is reading and mine is not; she must be a better parent than I am." Real Words: "Her son is reading and mine is not; some kids learn faster than other kids. We'll keep at it."

    b. **O**wned—is the comparison something that really belongs to you, or have you borrowed it from someone else? *Example*: After reading a magazine article, you tell yourself "I should make all our meals from scratch," as opposed to "I will serve healthy foods to my family." Hint: if you hear yourself using the word "should," chances are good it isn't really owned.

    c. **L**ife-enhancing—is the comparison enriching to your life or is it a weight around your neck? *Example*: "I will never leave my child in someone else's care," as opposed to "I will search for an appropriate caregiver for my child in order to refresh myself and be more able to care for my child."

    d. Flexible—is the comparison pliable and change-able or is it rigid and strict? *Example*: "I must always_____ and never _____" as opposed to "I will most often do _____, and carefully consider when I need to _____."

5. After the ROLF test, what changes will you make in your thoughts about comparison?

6. How will you remind yourself of these changes?

7. What or who do you need to say "no" to in your life?

8. Who can "lend" you strength to do what you need to do?

9. When will you contact this person?

    Date: _____ Time: _____

Ideas to take away with you

What's your "take-away" from coaching yourself through Comparison? Writing it down anchors the learning.

18

Finding Your
Parent-strengths

Think of a time when you were at your very best.

Such a moment stands out for me. Being eight years younger than my brother and five years younger than my sister, as a young child I often felt like my voice didn't have much influence. Paul and Janelle were older and I pretty much followed their lead. Until kindergarten that is...

One day on the playground, a new revelation dawned. Standing between the red metal, bumpy slide and the fast merry-go-round (not the kind with horses, but the kind straight out of a 1960s playground equipment catalog), I stood with four kids in a line to my left and four kids in a line to my right. The point of contention escapes me now, but they were toe to toe, each group wanting our play to go in specific and opposite directions. As the argument heated up, eight heads turned to me to make the decision and the awareness hit me: "I'm a leader!" Stepping into this newly discovered role, I brokered a compromise and, as I remember it, the contention ended.

As goofy as it sounds, I was at my very best in that moment in time. I doubt Arlene, Lennie, Shelly or Jim even remember the moment, but for me it was a watershed.

The Importance of parenting from strengths

As an adult, think about what it's like for you when you are working from non-strengths. For most people, it's draining and deadening. Tom Rath, number one New York Times Bestselling Author describes it in his book *StrengthsFinder 2.0* (2007):

> What happens when you're not in the 'strengths zone'? You're quite simply a very different person. In the workplace, you are *six times* less likely to be engaged in your job. When you're not able to use your strengths at work, chances are that you:
>
> • dread going to work
>
> • have more negative than positive interactions with your colleagues
>
> • treat your customers poorly
>
> • tell your friends what a miserable company you work for
>
> • achieve less on a daily basis
>
> • have fewer positive and creative moments.
>
> …[T]here are even more serious implications for your health and relationships if you're not in your strengths zone (Rath 2007, p.12).

Parenting is one of the most important jobs you hold. How might these same principles apply? Do you:

• dread going home?

- have more negative than positive interactions with your family?

- treat your children and spouse poorly?

- tell your friends what a difficult family you work with?

- achieve less on a daily basis?

- have fewer positive and creative moments?

To be clear, these applications are totally my conjecture, not Tom Rath's, but they are worth pondering.

Finding your strengths

How might living from your strengths impact your family life? Browse the List of Strengths below. Circle the word, if it has *ever* been true of you, even once. Don't over-think, just start circling.

Examples of talents and applications:

Advocate—an obvious strength: if you have a history of championing the disadvantaged, you've got a whole "toolbox" full of "tools" for effective use in campaigning for the needs of your child with autism/Asperger's.

Quizzical—study your child and ask yourself the obscure questions about his or her treatment that most people wouldn't think of.

Structured—a child with autism/Asperger's craves a structured environment—it's their safety net.

Leader—as I learned in Kindergarten, being a leader has benefited me greatly in treatment team meetings with professionals involved in my son's care. I always go in with a copied list of my son's accomplishments and my concerns for future

List of Strengths

A self-starter	A team builder	Accessible	A team player	Adaptable
Abiding	Absorbing	Analytical	Active	Assertive
Agreeable	An advocate	Brief	Animated	Burly
Astute	Aware	Capable	Bright	Cheerful
Busy-brained	Cagey	Classy	Changeable	Comfortable
Childlike	Chivalrous	Courageous	Coherent	Cultured
Connected	Cooperative	Diligent	Credible	Dependable
Dazzling	Deep	Easygoing	Delightful	Discreet
Detailed	Determined	Encouraging	Direct	Educated
Early	Earthy	Fearless	Economic	Entertaining
Efficient	Emotional	Friendly	Energetic	Flashy
Experienced	Fascinated	Gutsy	Festive	Fun-loving
Flowery	Fortunate	Hilarious	Functional	Harmonious
Funny	Gentle	Imaginative	Happy	Honorable
Healthy	Helpful	Internal	Honest	Industrious
Hospitable	Humorous	Kindhearted	Impartial	Invincible
Instinctive	Intense	Learned	Intuitive	Knowledgeable

Jolly
Known
Lively
Mature
Nostalgic
Organized
Pleasant
Protective
Receptive
Robust
Selective
Slow
Stimulating
Talented
Thrifty
Understood
Vivacious
Whimsical
Workable

Joyous
Lavish
Lovely
Merciful
Nurturing
Overt
Plucky
Quick
Reflective
Romantic
Sensitive
Somber
Strong
Tame
Tough
Unusual
Affectionate
Wild
Wry

Knowing
Leader
Level
Lucky
Nonchalant
Optimal
Placid
Premium
Quizzical
Resolute
Safe
Sincere
Spiritual
Successful
Tested
Typical
Verdant
Watchful
Zealous

Likeable
Lyrical
Nonstop
Organic
Plausible
Productive
Rambunctious
Ritzy
Scientific
Skillful
Steadfast
Succinct
Therapeutic
Unbiased
Victorious
Wealthy
Wistful
Zany

Loving
Neighborly
Offbeat
Peaceful
Political
Quiet
Reminiscent
Rural
Silly
Spicy
Structured
Tasteful
Tranquil
Upbeat
Warm-hearted
Willing
Young
Wise
Zippy

treatment. Since the beginning, I've assumed leadership in the treatment decisions. The professionals are a valuable resource, but Jordan's dad and I make the final decisions. Our attitude is not one of control, but rather matter-of-fact. Through the years, we've gotten some amazing services and resources by taking this stance.

Once you've discovered some of your natural abilities, how can you put them into practice? In his book, *Patterns of High Performance* Jerry Fletcher (1993, p.12) described two ways of getting results. (see Table)

Two Ways of Getting Results	
Grind-It-Out-Mode	**High-Performance Mode**
Aim for Predetermined Results	Aim for Better Than Expected Results
Hard Grinding Effort	Easy and Flowing
Exhausted and Relieved When It's Over	Energized and Wistful When It's Over

Fletcher asserts "high-performance mode generates outstanding results and enables [a person] to achieve much higher, more sustainable performance with less effort and less stress" (1993, p.13). Utilizing strengths brings energy to a project. For many, parenting an autism-impacted family means months and years of grinding it out. What might it be like to take a different perspective? To take your strengths and use them as tools to parent your family?

Math non-strength

I admit it, I am relational. I really like humans. Working with people is a strength of mine. Conversely, throughout my entire education, math has been a distinct "non-strength." Hey, let's just call it what it is—a weakness! I never unlocked the code of math. In graduate school, with clammy palms and racing heart, I opened the door to the most dreaded class of my life—statistics. Yuck. More than yuck. Would I be able to pass it? Would this class prevent me from getting my degree? I sincerely wondered if statistics would be the end of the road for my career.

Jerry Fletcher's principles saved me. My coach and I had previously discovered my high-performance plan and now working together created a "map" to develop my strengths with people and conquer the dreaded semester of statistics. I scheduled weekly tutoring sessions with a former high school math teacher who was also a friend. In the context of relationship, connection (and major workouts at the gym), I calmed my anxiety enough to actually learn statistics. Amazingly enough, I passed it no problem. Using my relational strengths, I conquered math for the first time in my life! Truly a modern-day miracle.

Coaching yourself through Finding Your Parent-strengths

1. Describe a time in your life when you were at your very best. This can be any experience, even one only significant to you though not neccesarily to others.

   ○ What was true about you in that moment?

   ○ What personal strengths did you access?

   ○ How did others respond to you working from your strengths?

   ○ How did you feel when you were at your very best?

   ○ What can you learn about yourself?

   For an even more effective exercise, write about three such incidents in detail.

2. Look over your list of personal strengths. What are your strengths?

   ○ Which strengths were easy to identify?

   ○ Which strengths surprise you?

   ○ Which strengths did you try to talk yourself out of?

3. What are you currently doing in "high-performance mode"?

4. What are you currently "grinding out"?

   ○ How can you develop your strengths to turn the grinding effort into more easy and flowing effort?

5. What are you going to do?

  Date: _____ Time: _____

  ○ Who do you know that could "tutor" you through this dilemma?

  ○ When will you contact this person?
    Date: _____ Time: _____

For more specific work on discovering your strengths, try the book *Strengthsfinder 2.0*, by Tom Rath (2007). It's an excellent resource based on 40 years of research and it's also a lot of fun!

Ideas to take away with you

What's your "take-away" from coaching yourself through Finding Your Parent-Strengths? Writing it down anchors the learning.

19

Parent Care

◇◇◇◇◇◇◇◇◇◇◇◇◇◇◇◇◇◇◇◇◇◇◇◇◇◇

"Your easiest most breeze-of-a-day as a parent of a child with autism is more stressful than my wildest, hardest, most difficult day *imaginable* as a medical doctor" (Knopf 2000). That's what Dr. Knopf said to me with a perfectly straight face.

Lola lived with that kind of stress as a single mom of nine-year-old Warren with Asperger's. Not only that, but her health was also in jeopardy. After surviving a difficult divorce, she wrestled with a bout of meningitis that almost killed her. (For more of their story, see Chapter 2: Outings.) Still in school to earn her teaching credential, she chipped away at the mountain of projects, knowing that self-care was crucial for a full recovery and long-term health. At one point she repeatedly studied for 40 minutes and napped for 20, just trying to get through her hours and days. Learning to sequence work and rest was a vital tool for managing stress and burnout. Lola's mantra? "I don't just want us to survive, I want us to thrive."

Lola survival tools

In order for that to happen, she absolutely, no-questions-asked, had to implement self-care into her life. The following are some nuggets of wisdom Lola has gathered over the past three years:

- Sometimes I can care for myself while sharing space and time with Warren; other times I can only care for myself while alone.

- It's OK to tell him I need to swim alone for 15 minutes or be in the garden alone for 20 while he's in the house.

- We have both needed to learn how to soothe ourselves.

- The point is me being *strong* enough to take time for myself.

- Trust is very important:

  ○ It's me trusting my child will be OK without me for 15 to 20 minutes.

  ○ It's my child trusting me that he can be on his own without my interaction for 15 to 20 minutes.

- My alone time teaches the boundary of "this is you" and "this is me."

- I now have tremendous freedom while in Warren's company.

- We can only learn to be together when we both feel safe emotionally.

- Being regularly involved in the right community has been the best way for both of us to feel safe emotionally.

- Community for Lola and Warren is synagogue, the local Herb Growers Society, and close friends. They provide the needed buoyancy and safety for us to really enjoy one another. *I ask you: what other group would give Warren his favorite birthday gift—ten gallons of loam herb-growing soil?*

- When we're in the middle of an intense interaction, each of us may need to either actively engage or take some meditative time. Respecting the needs of the other is essential.

Lola reports a recent event involving a disagreement in the car. Mom had made clear the way things needed to be and her son was not happy. Seeing their home down the road just a few blocks, she pulled over, telling Warren, "Because of your anger outburst, I don't feel safe in the car and can no longer talk successfully about this. Please get out and walk home. I'm unwilling to listen to the complaining, so while you're walking, please call someone else to talk about it." Harsh words? Not if you know Lola. She's a very involved, intuitive mom, but setting tough boundaries has been a sink or swim necessity for her. At this point, I'd say they are definitely not just surviving, but thriving.

Coach yourself through Parent Care

As a coach, I've worked with many autism-impacted families around the United States. Usually a parent starts coaching because of an urgent stuck spot. Once that issue is moved through, nine times out of ten, the next agenda item they choose turns out to be self-care.

1. In your more-stressful-than-a-doctor's life, what activities relax you? (Martindale 2008)

    ○ instant activities? (Example: deep breath, long drink of water, etc.)

    ○ free activities? (Example: hot bath, brisk walk, relaxation recordings, etc.)

    ○ under $5 activities? (Example: coffee out, buying a lottery ticket)

    ○ under $50 activities? (Example: manicure, pedicure, game of golf)

    ○ planned-for activities? (Example: a trip to the beach, a weekend away)

2. Which of these will you do this week?

3. What could stop you?

4. When will you do it? Date: _____ Time: _____

Hmmm… A question to ponder: How will taking care of your child's parent (in other words, YOU) benefit your child in the long run?

Ideas to take away with you

What's your "take-away" from coaching yourself through Parent Care? Writing it down anchors the learning.

20

What Fills *Your* Tank?

◇◇◇◇◇◇◇◇◇◇◇◇◇◇◇◇◇◇◇◇◇◇◇◇◇◇

A mom's story

Angela leaned on her kitchen sink, gathering strength to wash the dinner dishes and finish her day. The old yellow laminate of the counter was wiped clean of crumbs once again. Clean for now. Autism at her house seemed to be represented by crumbs. True, Collin was gaining skill, but oh so slowly. No matter how hard she tried, she couldn't keep up with the crumbs. Angela was tired. Tired of being tired.

The transition to kindergarten had been a tough one. Who could have known that leaving the early education classroom and leaping to the public school system would bring so much change? If *she* felt befuddled, how must Collin feel? If only he could tell her with words and not only with meltdowns.

The acronyms for services were new, the contact people and all of their phone numbers were new. The school was new, nice but very big and unfamiliar. Besides the many changes, grief was a companion these days. This wasn't what she had dreamed it would be to send her son to kindergarten. Five years ago holding him in the delivery room, a short, yellow bus was the farthest thing from her mind.

Angela's husband worked long hours. She was the on-duty parent from wake-up till bedtime, the center connecting all the spokes of the family wheel.

The family schedule included driving and participating in Collin's weekly occupational and speech therapy sessions. Angela's older son had soccer practice four times a week and games every weekend. In addition, Angela worked part-time, kept house, cooked for Collin's special diet and actively nurtured both of her boys.

Their life related closely to the findings of a research project which show that, "Children with special health care needs with autism spectrum disorder were more likely to live in families that report financial problems" *[Angela thinks, "check, that's us"]* "need additional income for the child's medical care," *[check]* "reduce or stop work because of the child's condition" *[check]* "spend [more than or equal to] 10 hours per week providing or coordinating care," *[check—more like 20-30 hours]* "and paid more than $1000 in the previous year for the child's care" *[check]* (Kogan *et al.* 2008, p.e1149). When would the raging exhaustion end?

An analogy

In Portland, Oregon, we have beautiful open reservoirs of city drinking water. A walk on the trails of Mt. Tabor Park leads you around landscaped, sparkling, huge pools of water. The sight really is breathtaking. My graduate school was within walking distance, and many times I walked out my stress on the hillside, breathing in the beauty.

Most years in Oregon, water is abundant with local rain and run-off from Mt. Hood snow. Occasionally, in the heat of

Restoration and Rejuvenation

What Energizes My Life?

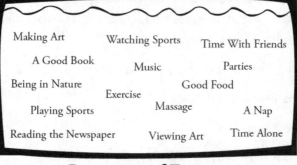

Making Art   Watching Sports   Time With Friends

A Good Book   Music   Parties

Being in Nature   Good Food

Exercise

Playing Sports   Massage   A Nap

Reading the Newspaper   Viewing Art   Time Alone

Reservoir of Energy

How often and how fully do I tap in to what
restores, rejuvenates, and fulfills me?

Where Does My Energy Go?

Personal Cup

(Martindale 2008a, artwork by Debi Vann,
Cherokee Design 2008.)

summer, even we Northwesterners have a drought and water lines drop at the Mt. Tabor Reservoirs.

In the diagram Restoration and Rejuvenation, notice the Reservoir of Energy. It is filled by energy-giving activities. When asked, "What fills *your* tank?" answers, from people I have worked with are diverse:

- "Training and competing in triathlons"
- "Reading a good book"
- "Tae Kwon Do"
- "A hot bath with candles"
- "Marathons"
- "Soothing music"
- "Classic Rock n' Roll"
- "Libraries"
- "Poker night"
- "Shopping"
- "Exercise"
- "Chocolate"
- "Time alone"
- "Time with people"
- "Playing sports"
- "Watching sports"
- "A massage"
- "Yoga"

- "Art"

- "Good food"

- "Nature"

- "A walk around the Mt. Tabor Reservoirs"

- "Good coffee".

In the diagram, note the reservoir has a valve on the side which is at all times depleting the energy supply, just like the drinking water reservoirs. If the tank is not replenished regularly, it will run dry.

The attached hosepipe drains energy into the Personal Cup, a smaller container with multiple faucets. For most parents of children with autism, the faucets are full-open with energy coursing out continually. "Gallons" of energy are required to get through moments and days. Over time the cup empties. This is where Angela found herself, exhausted, surrounded by crumbs and with both containers on the dregs.

Coach yourself through
What Fills *Your* Tank?

Draw your Reservoir of Energy.

1. What energizes your life? Writing these down in the "reservoir" will anchor the learning. Include large and small activities, for example a road trip or taking a deep breath.

    a. What else energizes you?

    b. What rejuvenates you?

    c. What fulfills you?

    d. What energized you in the years before you were a parent?

    e. Write down as many as you can.

Draw your Personal Cup.

2. Where does your energy go? Be specific, for example driving to appointments, or managing the paperwork for my child's care.

3. Draw a faucet for each one. Which faucets take the most energy?

4. Looking over your list of "faucets", after each one, place the words "yes/no" and ask yourself, "Is it choice-ful? i.e. Is this "faucet" something I'm choosing to do or is it a requirement? Think carefully—sometimes activities that feel like requirements really are choices.

5. Which faucet's flow can you slow down? Which faucet(s) can you turn off completely?

Draw the connecting hose and valve.

1. How often do you tap into the things that restore, rejuvenate and fulfill you?

2. How *fully* do you tap into the things that restore, rejuvenate and fulfill you?

3. How can you turn the valve fully open?

4. How can you make it "luscious"? In other words, make the restoration activity as "filling" as possible. Example: reading the newspaper for ten minutes in your most comfortable chair with your favorite music playing.

5. What can you do for five minutes?

6. What will you do?

7. When will you do it? Day: _____ Time: _____

8. Who can give support for you to do what you need to do?

A word about addictions

All of these examples are, of course, fine when used in moderation, but some could become addictions with harmful consequences. It's important to notice when an activity is moving from being one that fills your tank to one that creates a hole in your tank, rapidly draining it:

-   Are you using the activity or substance more and more exclusively as the only escape mechanism?

-   Is the behavior or substance (food, coffee, cigarettes, alcohol, etc.) giving you a feeling of high or well-being that you find difficult to replicate with anything else?

- Are harmful consequences happening or could they happen from your level of use or activity?

- Is the level of use of your activity removing other positives in your life or negating their benefits?

Examples:

  ○ financial losses from poker or shopping

  ○ cluttering of the home due to shopping

  ○ injury from over-exercising

  ○ difficulty sleeping due to excessive caffeine intake

  ○ obesity and other health problems from use of food

  ○ problems in relationships due to your use or activity.

If you answer "yes" to any of these questions (even if you answer, "uh, maybe") there is a good chance your water tank has a hole in it and what feels like nourishment is really set to destroy you. Now is the time to seek help through an addictions hot-line, a professional counselor and/or your personal physician. That niggling in your gut? Listen to it!

What will you do? When? Date: _____ Time: _____

Ideas to take away with you

What's your "take-away" from coaching yourself through What Fills *Your* Tank? Writing it down anchors the learning.

21

I'm a Dad,
What Can *I* Do?"

As a kid and through early adult life, Damon loved sports, especially basketball. He served a stint in the Navy and got married as he describes "later in life" to Lauren. With a low chuckle, he pronounces they both came from "checkered backgrounds" and wanted to provide a different growing-up experience for their own kids. (Until age 24, the longest he ever lived in one place was four years on the Navy ship the USS *Clark*.)

One dad's story

He explains his journey of being dad to his boy, Chad—now a hand-shaking, hilarious, considerate, sharp fifth-grader—who was diagnosed on the autism spectrum at age six. Damon was "not even aware [when] it started, but suddenly there it was." Chad didn't really like being held as a baby except when being swung. So Dad swung him and swung him, singing to his son in his self-described "lousy, but low droning voice."

The toddler had a "big head with a smallish body," and his speech was somehow different from other people's. When the family moved into a new house, Chad said his first word, which wasn't "Mama" or "Dada." He toddled into the kitchen, pointed and said "ball." Damon was both startled and delighted. Always the teaching father, he explained to his son that the big square thing humming in the room was not a "ball" but a "refrigerator." Chad insisted on "ball," however, took two steps backward and pointed at a golf ball lodged between the icebox and the wall. He alone had noticed it out of the corner of his eye.

As Chad grew, Mom and Dad could see he was unique.

When Chad reached kindergarten, Damon decided sports must surely be the answer and enrolled his boy in a local basketball program. But the noisier the games got, the more Chad withdrew. He would dash to the location with fewest people— center court—and run in circles. Dad was displeased with this clearly "intentional," unsportsmanlike behavior and was determined to teach his son about teamwork.

It all came to a head on a game day with Chad firmly pronouncing, "Dad, I *really* don't want to play anymore." Dad describes taking on "man-thinking" while he laid down the law and pulled out the classic lecture on personal responsibility: "You can't leave your teammates down; they're depending on you!" In retrospect, Damon readily admits he didn't understand what was really going on. His lecture only escalated the situation at game time. Afterwards, he had "no idea what to think." Scouring the internet, searching for symptoms, he found "a million things it could be."

Meanwhile the family was struck with agonizing tragedy. Chad's baby sister Sage died of Sudden Infant Death Syndrome. Just "keeping [their] feet moving" was all he and Lauren could do. The parents definitely saw patterns developing in Chad's "talking-at-you" relational style, but didn't know what it all meant.

The following year, Chad's first grade teacher recommended he be tested for autism/Asperger's at Oregon Health and Sciences University. Behind a one-way mirror, Damon describes watching his son solve puzzles that "would be hard for *me* to figure out." At the same time, Chad was "talking at" the psychologist about an earth science TV show while rarely looking at the puzzle.

At the end of the grueling day, the professional team diagnosed Chad as having Asperger's, a syndrome on the autism spectrum. At first, Damon bristled, "No he doesn't!" His perception of autism was children who don't speak. As the doctor described their findings, Damon says "my pieces came together." All the little idiosyncrasies and peculiarities were connected under one umbrella. "It was really hard. We both cried," Damon reports still with a twinge of sadness.

"At first, we didn't like the diagnosis. We wanted something to fix it—we wanted *him* fixed." Damon spent hours in late night and early morning research and reading, convinced "something was lacking." Maybe their son needed more exercise, different food, additional vitamin supplements. "We tried everything." Chad "seemed happier" with the omega supplements, but nothing "fixed" him. Nothing took away the Asperger's. "Gradually our thought process changed."

Recently, when a new assistant was introduced to the social skills group, Damon took her aside saying, "Chad is not broken and he doesn't need to be fixed." He further explained that his son has "some really incredibly great strengths," is extremely considerate and wants more than anything to meet people and make new friends. Dad also articulated that Chad had some real challenges to work at including remembering not to talk "at" people, but "with" them.

Damon's suggestions

Damon's suggestions for dads with autism-impacted kids?

1. Think of yourself as "coach," a position which includes:

    ○ How to motivate.

    ○ How to stand up to resistance.

    ○ When to back down.

    ○ The "drills"—Damon asserts "Free-throws don't come naturally." Even pro players have free-throw drills as a part of their practice regime. Keep teaching your child how and why to do the social thing. Say to them:

    ○ "This is how we shake hands with people."

    ○ "This is why we look them in the eye."

    ○ "Here's how you give hugs."

2. "Be prepared, your kid is going to want to please you in some way." Study your child's talents and help them craft the talent into something that will be truly helpful. Keep thinking of your child as an "actor" or a "spy" who has to fit in from an outsider's perspective. Break it down and teach the little things he or she needs to know. Make it fun.

3. Your kid's going to be a nerd! Not everyone has to be a suave, smooth-talking salesman. What's important is that they be the best they can. As one person with Asperger's once quipped: "The NTs caused global warming and we Aspies are the ones who will fix it!"

4. Coaching has to take place now! I won't always be here. There's no waiting to get involved in my kid's life. Damon and Lauren live by this principle every day of their lives in parenting Chad and his five-year-old spunky sister, Autumn.

Dr. William Bolman suggests the following ways in which dads can be actively involved with their children impacted by autism (Bolman 2006, p.2):

- doing [discreet trial] exercises

- generalization of skills learned in school or home settings

- getting the autism-impacted child more active

- helping with structure, limit-setting and discipline

- assisting with homework and reading to their children

- best yet, by sharing the horrendous workload that [many] moms carry in treatment responsibilities, [husbands can help] wives get some break time to relax, regroup and perhaps even to feel better!

Moms, this bullet point is *not* to be photocopied 50 times, highlighted and left all around the house as a way to beg your husband to be more helpful! It's merely a suggestion for dads to consider. Although, dads, the moms are probably thinking, "Please, oh, please do consider it!"

When the inevitable "time-bomb" of adolescence hits, dads have a tactical opportunity to impact their son or daughter and launch them into adulthood, regardless of the severity of autism/Asperger's. To these dads, Dr. Bolman asserts

Dealing with adolescence. As autistic children become teenagers, at least three new issues appear – [1] sexual development... in a just world, the issue of masturbation [with boys] should be handled by dads*...[2] tantrums become potentially dangerous as the child gets bigger and stronger, and [3] a new set of educational issues is needed to deal with the transition from the school to community—to a world in which practical knowledge, the ability to communicate, and street skills are essential... For example autistic-based aggression toward moms needs much more than autism consultants and skills trainers, and the post-high school world of the community (Bolman 2006, p.1).

Dads, you are needed in your family. Whether you are married or single, don't short-change the importance of your influence. Even little bits of involvement can make a difference that lasts a lifetime.

---

*   An excellent resource for puberty-related issues is the book by Mary J. Wrobel (2003) *Taking Care of Myself: A Healthy Hygiene, Puberty and Personal Curriculum for Young People with Autism*. Future Horisons, Arlington, Texas.

Coach yourself through "I'm a Dad, What Can *I* Do?"

1. In what area does your son/daughter need a coach?

2. How will you motivate?

3. How will you stand up to resistance?

4. When will you know it's time to back down?

5. What "drills" can you put in place?

6. How can you make the drills fun?

7. How can you make the drills meaningful?

8. How can you make the drills memorable?

9. What will you do?

10. When will you do it? Day: _____ Time: _____

11. How will you congratulate your son/daughter when they finish the drill?

12. How will you congratulate yourself?

Ideas to take away with you

What's your "take-away" from coaching yourself through "I'm a Dad, what can *I* Do?"? Writing it down anchors the learning.

22

Marriage Building

⟨∞∞∞∞∞∞∞∞∞∞∞∞∞∞∞∞∞∞∞∞∞∞∞∞∞∞∞∞∞∞∞∞⟩

Standing at the altar. Saying "I do." Imagining…what?
If you're like most people you might be thinking…

- Nothing's going to get in our way."

- "I will love this woman through *all* things."

- "He's so involved I'll always respect this man."

- "We make such a great team!"

- "We are eternal soul-mates."

Later, autism/Asperger's knocks on your door. And you'll never forget how you were told.

After the stun of the diagnosis, the sheer workload can feel undo-able to a couple. Add the extra expenses that always come with autism/Asperger's, and intact marriages are shaken to the core. Unceasing stress. (C'mon, for better or worse?)

Research is confirming what many autism-impacted couples hoped was untrue, that having a child on the autism spectrum actually *decreases* the odds of living in a higher income household, even after accounting for the level of parents' education, type of family, parents' age, location of the household and minority ethnicity. Autism-impacted families earn—*hold your breath*—14 percent less than comparable households without autism at their house (Montes and Halterman 2008a, p.e821). Evidence points to ASD childcare issues directly impacting employment for both mothers and fathers to the extent that one or both need to work part-time (Montes and Halterman 2008a). The socioeconimic factor alone places extreme pressure on most marriages. (Please, not this kind of for richer or poorer?)

Seasons of functioning

Under the best of circumstances, becoming parents is usually a bumpy transition. Suddenly, the mom is fully on board as a parent, being physiologically required to give birth, heal and get hormonally rebalanced while meeting many of the physical needs of the baby. Most of her discretionary attention, which was previously focused on the husband, is abruptly diverted towards the child. The season of life is rapidly changed. Often the husband feels displaced with an occasional rivalry developing between husband and baby (Wenzel 2008).

Dr. David Wenzel of River Ridge Counseling in Sandy, Oregon, invites couples to consider that in every life and in every marriage, there are seasons of functioning. The current situation *will* change. The only constant in life *is* change. Kids develop and grow—even kids with autism. Skill levels increase. Solutions appear. Financial circumstances modify. If the current season is blizzarding, "don't pine for the motorcycle, go skiing" (Wenzel 2008). Meaning, look around at your life. Ask yourself, "What is there to enjoy?" Find it. Do it. Celebrate it.

Moms and dads

A dad's experience of raising a child with autism is often very different from a mom's experience. And that difference can create a chasm too great to bridge. Reported divorce rates for autism-impacted families in the US vary widely, anywhere from 40 to 90 percent.

How does divorce happen? In 2006, child psychiatrist William M. Bolman, MD reported his observations of a typical autism-impacted family cycle: "[I]nevitably normal family structure and balance became focused around the needs of the child with autism. Thus, marital relationship time disappeared and with it went the sharing, mutuality, and working out of joint issues that promote marital survival" (Bolman 2006, p.1). Parents of children with autism often find themselves taking on a divide-and-conquer strategy. Granted, not all families have a traditional constellation, and the following quote may not apply to you. Please know my intent is not to exclude or to endorse a specific agenda, but rather to shed some light on a pattern experienced by hundreds of thousands of autism-impacted families: "Dads [go] to work and [earn] money while moms [stay] at home and [try] to become experts on autism! The inevitable result is growing apart, not together" (Bolman 2006, p.1). Sound familiar? I've heard the story hundreds of times.

This set-up can work for a few years, but in Dr. Bolman's experience inevitably

> Dads [become] frustrated at the demands of their wives to 'play with' a son or daughter who [doesn't] know how to play, and moms [become] frustrated at the lack of involvement of their mates. In retrospect, this appears to be the time that the existing intra-marital separation

starts the couples on a path towards formal separation and divorce. (Bolman 2006, p.2).

Some mothers go even further, to the point of unhealthy, taking on the role of Super-Mom Autism Expert—can't you just see her with a blue cape and a red and gold "S" on her shirt? We women have probably all been occasionally tempted to take on her persona. At the same time, some fathers lose themselves in being the Super Provider, buckling down to work even harder for the family while two "good people...head off in different life directions. There is no question that this role division is effective for a few years, but one of the things that keeps marriages together is deeply shared interests" (Bolman 2006). Marriage needs time together, sharing mutual enjoyment and working through challenges as a team.

Marriage researcher, Dr. John Gottman has studied happy marriages for over 20 years at the University of Washington where he identified the primary characteristic of a long-term, satisfying marriage is the foundation of *friendship*. And, more particularly, a friendship where you think positively about your spouse. It sounds so simple, yet there is something very powerful in what he calls the "Positive Perspective." The strong base of friendship in marriage is broken down into the first four levels of what he calls The Sound Marital House (Gottman 2004):

1. Knowing each other and periodically updating knowledge.

2. Cultivating fondness and admiration which is the antidote of contempt, a marriage killer.

3. Developing the habit of turning towards each other versus turning away.

4. Making the previous three so much a part of your thinking, that your first thoughts of your spouse are automatically positive (Gottman 2004, p.48).

In case you're not convinced at the importance of friendship and positive regard in marriage, Gottman adds: "There was a surprise in this work. It also appears from our clinical work that these first four levels...are related to romance, passion, and good sex in marriage" (Gottman 2004, p.48). Cultivating a problem-solving friendly partnership has many benefits!

For further exploration of this process, his book *The Seven Principles for Making Marriage Work* (Gottman 1999) is easy reading with fun, not-too-intense exercises to strengthen your own "Sound Marital House."

So standing on this side of the altar, and on this side of the autism diagnosis, what is there to enjoy? Find it. Do it. Celebrate it.

How can you begin making better out of worse... together?

Coach yourself through Marriage Building

1. Where would you rate your marriage today? Rate it on a scale of 0–10 with 0 being completely disconnected while living separate lives, and 10 being connected and working seamlessly as a team.

2. What can you do today to raise it by 0.5 (or 0.25)?

3. Where would you like it to be in six months?

4. How would you describe the "season" you are in as parents in your marriage?

5. What are the benefits of this season?

6. What is one thing to enjoy in this season individually? As a couple?

7. What resources can you access to assist in your marriage? Example: Gottman's book, going on a weekend away, hiring a relationship coach, seeking counseling, etc.

8. What will you do today?

9. Who will hold you accountable to do what you say you're going to do?

10. How will you know you are on the right track?

11. How will you and your spouse celebrate the small changes in your marriage?

Ideas to take away with you

What's your "take-away" from coaching yourself through Marriage Building? Writing it down anchors the learning.

23

For Husbands

✕✕✕✕✕✕✕✕✕✕✕✕✕✕✕✕✕✕✕✕✕✕✕✕✕✕✕✕✕

Written in collaboration with
David M. Wenzel, Ph.D.

Dave Wenzel is a professor, professional counselor, happily married man, dad of six kids and marathon runner. Many of Dave's colleagues and friends—like me—don't get the marathon thing. What kind of kook purposely bangs up his body to run 26 miles and 385 yards? I mean, fitness is one thing. Give me a health club, but a marathon? Why put yourself through it? All of you marathon runners and iron men please forgive me. There is something in it of great value which I don't comprehend.

Marathon running is a true metaphor for married dads of a child with autism/Asperger's. Being that kind of dad is a tough job. Staying on the same team with your wife and sharing together the challenges is even tougher. Ever say to yourself "Wait a minute, this wasn't part of the 'for better or worse' contract"? It takes a rational, behavioral choice to stay in the race.

Clearly, in your "marathon" of life, your "track" is tougher than most of the other runners. Your race is in 100 degrees heat, uphill, with a 50 mph wind in your face. You could choose to slip out of the race and into a pub at Mile 8. Who would blame you?

When your legs are iron and your mouth is sandpaper and quitting seems like the best option, you ask yourself, "Why am I out here? Why am I doing this?" The answer: "Oh, yeah. Mile 26" (Wenzel 2008).

You *could* stop at any time. You *could* drop into the pub and maybe find people who were more attentive and understanding to your needs.

But you will never experience the benefits of crossing the finish line. Dave the marathoner says, "The intimacy that comes from having worked through a problem [in marriage] is very different than the intimacy of a temporary sexual encounter. There's a…physical and emotional connection that comes *only* through problem solving" (Wenzel 2008).

You could stop. But you'd miss out on the Mile 26 celebration, with the gut-level satisfaction of completing the race. You'd give up the celebration of having made it through and the camaraderie of joining your friends and your spouse at the pub. Dave says crossing the marathon finish line "is like trying to describe a color to someone. You just can't imagine it unless you've done it" (Wenzel 2008).

So how do you stay for the long haul? Here's what Dave says who, by the way, stayed to the end with his first wife through a very long and difficult illness:

- Be willing to say, "I am angry about this."

- Acknowledge the anger, frustration, exasperation and resentment. If you don't, it will eat you alive before you even realize it.

- Bear in mind if you duck out early, you'll lose the opportunity of truly celebrating your success.

- Recognize your wife *will* give the kids more attention, particularly with a special needs child.

- There is a central need for both parents to remain adult. Mothers are the ones who give unconditional attention, love and acceptance. Adults shouldn't expect those qualities from each other.

- Recognize that you can't have *all of* what you want in life, but you can have *some of* what you want. Perhaps for now, you can have only *a little bit.*

- The current situation is not always how it will be. People figure things out. Children grow—even children with autism/Asperger's. This season *will* change.

- There are seasons of functioning, so enjoy what you have now. In the winter, "don't pine for the motorcycle, go skiing."

- Negotiation is *energy* in a relationship.

- There is unimaginable physical and emotional intimacy that comes from moving towards your wife and problem solving together. To this most women would say a resounding, *"AMEN!"* (Wenzel 2008).

True marathon runners know something that a marathon cheater will never know—the indescribable sensation of crossing the finish line at Mile 26 having run every aching, rewarding step of the race!

Coach yourself through For Husbands

Some of the following questions are taken from the book *Co-active Coaching* (Whitworth, Kimsey-House and Sandahl 1998 pp.21–22).

1. Where do you want to make a difference in your life?

2. What do you value most in your relationship with your wife?

3. What works for you when you are successful at making changes?

4. Where do you usually get stuck?

5. What motivates you when you get stuck?

6. How do you deal with disappointment or failure?

7. How are you about doing what you say you'll do?

8. This week, how will you "stay in the race"?

9. What is your action? (Or what will you do?)

10. When will you do it? Day: _____ Time: _____

11. Who on your "team" will know about your action to cheer you on?

Ideas to take away with you

What's your "take-away" from coaching yourself through For Husbands? Writing it down anchors the learning.

24

Single Parenting

⟡⟡⟡⟡⟡⟡⟡⟡⟡⟡⟡⟡⟡⟡⟡⟡⟡⟡⟡⟡⟡⟡⟡⟡⟡⟡⟡⟡⟡⟡

Portions of this book were written from the inspiring location of Mount Angel Abbey, St. Benedict, Oregon. The day I recall is the best Oregon has to offer: September, sunny, green as far as the eye can see, finches feeding and the sound of nearby water. We web-footed Oregonians try to make the rest of the world think it rains here all the time so we can enjoy our beauty in peace. Wink, wink!

Two single moms

After in-town errands took longer than anticipated and taking several wrong turns, I was delayed getting here Friday evening. Late for dinner, yes, but just in time to see a mother deer and her two fawns. They stopped me in my hurrying tracks, as the three of them nibbled on the grass of an athletic field. Later one of the monks told me "that is where she trains her children." I watched, captivated.

As a newly single mom myself, I related to this mama doe. She was taking care of her family's need for nourishment *and* she was fully on duty. A car door slammed in the distance and her head was up, on alert. The babies kept eating, unaware of her watchfulness. She had her danger-radar on and they did not. They didn't need to, they were children and she was the adult. Slowly, she moved herself between her brood and the direction of the noise, just in case.

Yes, Mama Doe, I am like you. I feel the constant weight of watchfulness.

She wasn't panicky. When the church bells rang, she didn't flinch. No danger in the familiar, thunderous sound. One fawn wandered deep into the soccer goal. Apparently the grass was greener on the inside of the net. I wondered how he would get out. She watched him, but only watched. He did get a bit confused, nuzzled around a bit, but then easily found the front opening. She went back to her own dinner. While leading her children to the most succulent grass available, she also looked after her own needs. She ate while her children ate.

Yes, Mama Doe, I am like you. I watch my kids try new things and wonder if and when intervention will be needed. Like you, I would take a bullet for them and I also know that taking care of my needs helps my family in the long run.

The most striking thing about this single-mom deer? She was beautiful. She was competent, curious and calm which made for a graceful beauty. And she was strong.

Oh, how I want to be like you, Mama Doe.

Coach yourself through Single Parenting

An effective model of health under recent discussion (Ivey *et al.* 2005) focuses on five spheres crucial to personal wellness. And wellness contributes to both longevity and quality of life. The following list is a much-abbreviated version of their conclusions:

1. **creative sphere**—includes areas such as thinking, emotions, work and positive humor

2. **coping**—leisure, stress management, self-worth, realistic beliefs

3. **social**—friendship, love

4. **essential**—spirituality, cultural identity, self-care

5. **physical**—exercise, nutrition.

   - In your life, which of the five categories is most in need of attention?

   - Which category will you focus on now?

   - Of that category, which sub-topic stands out to you? Example: Category: 3. social—sub-topic: friendship

   - What's missing in this area?

   - When was a time, if ever, that you had more of it in your life?

   - At that time, what did you do to successfully cultivate it?

   - Here and now, what's the next step towards gaining more of it in your life?

- If your answer is "I don't know," close your eyes and take three slow, deep breaths.

- If you did know, what would you know?

- How will you enhance your focus point this week?

- When will you do it? Date: _____ Time: _____

- How will you enhance your focus point today?

- What time? _____

Ideas to take away with you

What's your "take-away" from coaching yourself through Single Parenting? Writing it down anchors the learning.

25

Laugh a Little

Autism at our house means the same joke is funny every time! Always told with the same vocal inflections, here's one we've laughed at for 14 years:

Person 1: I had a headache and called the doctor. He told me to take two aspirin and a hot bath.

Person 2: Well (pause), what happened?

Person 1: I took the two aspirin (pause) but I couldn't finish drinking (pause) the hot bath!

Diana and Jack

Jack has high-functioning autism. For more of their story, see Chapter 15: Fairness.

Diana writes: Last spring at the dinner table, Jack shared a story. At school that day, during an all-fifth-grade activity, he was assigned a seat next to a boy from another class. Jack had been oblivious to the young man the entire year, but this time he introduced himself in his typical outgoing manner, "Hi, I'm Jack." The student's name was Cory. After some small talk Jack noticed this young man's hand looked different with only three fingers. Jack asked him about it and Cory explained he was born with the disability. Without missing a beat Jack said "That's OK, everyone has 'adaptions' like me—I have autism."

I (Mom) was surprised by the empathy, compassion and honesty he demonstrated at that moment. It really touched my heart and provided a unique window into how Jack deals with his own challenges.

The story opened up a good discussion around the dinner table that night about everyone having some type of "adaption" or challenge. I innocently asked Jack what he thought was Dad's adaption? He jumped out of his chair and around the table corner to put his hand on Dale's head exclaiming "Dad, you're bald"! After I got over my laughter I asked him what he thought my adaption was. Much to my delight he stared at me for a moment and was silent. Ahhh…the joy of being perfect in your child's eyes. Autism, I love it.

Damon and Chad

Chad has been diagnosed with Asperger's. For more of their story see Chapter 21: I'm a Dad, What Can *I* Do?

Damon writes: When a third grade classmate invited him to an end of the year swimming party, Chad thought he had arrived socially, because on TV only the "cool kids" go to pool parties.

Not a strong swimmer, Chad armed himself with water wings and strategically placed flotation devices in the pool, preparing to go down the slide. I (Dad) had no concerns. Apparently, neither did my son.

Chad is a bit uncoordinated with large feet for his age. As he methodically navigated the slide's ladder, other parents watched with concern. He seemed hesitant and unsure as he climbed. Several parents muttered in my direction, "Maybe he shouldn't be doing that," and "He doesn't have to do this if he doesn't want to." The other kids noticed the cue and told Chad it was OK *not* to go down the slide. No reply from Chad as he climbed.

When finally seated at the top of the slide, Chad turned to me at pool's edge.

"Dad, if I don't make it tell Mom I love her."

This had an odd effect on the crowd. Half of them suppressed a laugh, and the other half were hushed. Not one to miss an opportunity to be a smart aleck, I said "Chad, what about me, your father?"

Chad paused, looked at me, and without missing a beat said, "Dad, if I don't make it…tell your wife I love her." And he shot down the slide into the pool.

Amy and AJ

AJ has been diagnosed with Asperger's. Read more of their story in Chapter 5: "Invisible" Autism and Chapter 8: Sleeplessness.

Amy writes: Two weeks before AJ turned two, he decided to empty out all the drawers in his large oak dresser which he promptly climbed. The result was the dresser falling back on top of him pinning him to the ground and I (Mom—seven months pregnant) almost giving birth out of sheer fright for AJ. The toddler didn't shed a tear even with this huge piece of furniture on him. Adrenaline racing, I flung the dresser with one arm and quickly checked him over. He had minor abrasions to his face and chest, but I wanted an expert opinion and rushed him to the ER to insure that he hadn't broken any ribs or worse. Eloquent in complex sentences by 18 months, AJ reported it "hurt to breathe."

After the doctor found no broken bones, he wanted to see if my son was aware enough to answer questions. During the check-up, AJ had been impressing the doctor and staff with his vast knowledge of construction trucks and equipment: front loader, dump truck, track-hoe, etc. The doctor pointed out that he forgot to mention the bulldozer, to which AJ replied, "I know about bulldozers, but I like to call them 'Boogie-Boog-Boogs' instead."

This of course got the doctor laughing, so to test him even further, he asked AJ how old he would be on his next birthday. AJ looked up at him with his big brown eyes and oinked twice like a little pig!

The doctor turned to me and said, "I think he'll be fine, Mrs. Southfield."

Ramona and Jacob

Jacob was diagnosed with classic autism at the age of three.

It started off as not one bit funny. That's how Ramona tells it. At a family reunion, her son Jacob was bullied by a dog. Yes, a dog. (See Chapter 10: Bullying for an apt definition.)

Preparing for family reunions was always an immense undertaking for the autism-impacted branch of the Perez family. A big clan of origin made for lots of aunts, uncles and a whole tribe of cousins. The Northwest gathering house was small and rain was frequent, which meant a load of people tucked into a small space.

Historically, Jacob (age 7) had struggled at these get-to-gethers. His extended family loved him, but weren't sure what to do with him. A few uncles checked in and discovered connection points of spinning and tickling him. Most relatives just gave him a lot of space. Ramona occasionally discovered a crying auntie grieving over her nephew's aloneness. All in all, the atmosphere was loud, energetic and unpredictable—lots of fun, but not the ideal recipe for a child with autism.

One more voice in the cacophony was Bongo the extremely smart, black poodle. When asserting himself or defending his territory with most of the Perez kinfolk, Bongo was quickly put in his place. Ramona felt like she could read Bongo's mind: That Jacob kid, he's different. He's a weaker member of the pack. I may be below most of these chumps, but I'm definitely above him and will never let him forget it. This is my house, kid, and my job is to torment you!!

And torment he did. Bongo repeatedly cornered Jacob, snarling and growling with no mercy. The dog would go looking for the boy as if trying to get a reaction out of him. And the pooch's strategy worked, getting a huge screaming meltdown reaction every time. What power!

Ramona and her husband requested Bongo be kept in a separate room, but with dozens of people opening and closing doors, inevitably the poodle would get out, hunt Jacob down and persecute him. It was a long four days for the boy and his parents. Driving into their own driveway was a welcome relief. Home.

Recovery time for Jacob was always planned for in advance. After each family gathering and usually for several days, he let off steam with lots of flapping, screeching and pacing. It was expected. At bedtime the first night, however, the barking started. It was his protest. He didn't want to go to bed, so he barked at Mom and Dad. At school, he barked at his teachers.

At his after-school daycare, he barked at other children. At home, when his little brother bugged him, Jacob barked at him. Standing in the store check-out line, he barked at the customers. Bongo had left his mark.

Jacob's parents, teachers and daycare created a concerted plan with common language to combat the barking. For two weeks, the barking continued. During that time, the dog-tired Ramona called her friend Kathy. After hearing the full story from beginning to end, Kathy replied, "It really is sad that the dog bullied Jacob and that he had such a hard time." Then she hesitated, "But really, when you think about it, it's quite funny that Jacob is barking at people all over town!" And she burst out laughing!

For Ramona, the greatest gift she could have been given at the moment was just that—laughter. In fact, Ramona started laughing, almost fell off her chair and kept laughing until tears were streaming down her face!

Kathy asked, "Does he really sound like a poodle?"

"Yes, it's a very life-like imitation."

And the heaving laughter started again on both sides of the phone.

Coach yourself through Laugh a Little

1. What does autism look like at your house?

2. What are some quirky things that have happened?

3. Without making fun of your child, how can you re-frame the quirkiness into a humorous story?

4. Where will you write down the story? (Example: a journal, computer, etc.)

5. Who is a safe person you can share the funny story with?

6. How can you make humor a regular part of your life?

Ideas to take away with you

What's your "take-away" from coaching yourself through Laugh a Little? Writing it down anchors the learning.

Appendix 1:

Note to Grandparents

Do you ache watching your children struggle in the great effort of parenting a child with autism or Asperger's? You worked hard and trained your kids well to be responsible adults, wanting them to have rich, full, meaningful, rewarding lives. The life they live is extremely challenging, every day. You admire their strength and tenacity, respect their stamina and wish you could somehow take away the pain like you could when they were little.

You are among millions of grandparents who share similar feelings. The epidemic of autism impacts all generations, in all income brackets, in all countries.

I overhear this pain in the strangest places: two women walking on treadmills at the health club, a group of red-hatted ladies at the coffee shop, the woman in the chair next to me getting a pedicure, or the couple in the waiting area of the tire store. Parents are gravely concerned for their adult children with autism-impacted families. Hopeless is the usual theme:

- "How can I help?"

- "I feel so useless."

- "My daughter is overtired; I'm really concerned for her."

- "My son works 60 hours a week just to pay for the extra therapies."

- "My step-daughter has two kids on the autism spectrum!"

This coach's biggest suggestion: *support health*.

As much as you want to, you can't take the load away completely. It's there and your children's characters are being strengthened day by day carrying it. But, you can support health in little and big ways.

Turn to Appendix 4: How Can I Help to coach yourself on supporting health.

Parent Checklist: Ready for a Coach?

Circle the numbers applying to you

1. I'm new to this autism/Asperger's stuff and don't know where to start.

2. I've gathered lots of autism/Asperger's information and would like someone to "hold a space" for me to sort, discover and decide.

3. I'm stuck!

4. I feel overwhelmed with managing my child's care.

5. I want to move from just coping to hoping.

6. I'm willing to receive input from someone else.

7. My family and I want to move forward as a cohesive unit.

8. I want to ensure I parent each of my children well.

9. Parenting my child with ASD looks like it's going to be a long-haul trip for me and I want to strive for health and balance.

10. I'm ready to work together to accomplish bigger than big goals!

11. I want to embrace life as an opportunity for great meaning and purpose.

12. Bring it on! I'm motivated. Let's get going. Three months from now, I want my life to be different.

If you answered "yes" to 3 or more contact a coach who specializes in autism/Asperger's.

(Adapted from Cresswell, Miller and Thomas, 2005)

Ruth Knott Schroeder, MA, ACC
17150 University Ave, Suite 101
Sandy, OR 97055
USA
www.copetohope.com

Checklist for Choosing a Coach

〰〰〰〰〰〰〰〰〰〰〰〰〰〰〰〰〰〰〰〰〰〰〰〰〰〰〰〰〰〰〰〰

- Visit www.copetohope.com (Ruth Knott Schroeder's coaching website), www.coachfederation.org or www. westerncoaches.net to find a well-trained coach. (Websites accessed 29 January 2009.)

- Be diligent in asking the coach if they have been specifically trained in coaching skills.

- Does he or she currently hold or is in the process of acquiring an International Coach Federation (ICF) credential? Visit www.coachfederation.org to learn more about the stellar ethical and experience standards of ICF coaches.

- Don't be misled into thinking a coach is a competent coach because they have other professional credentials or set high fees.

- Ask them about their experience with the autism spectrum/Asperger's syndrome.

- Request an interview session.

- Ruth recommends conducting interview sessions with two to three coaches before making a decision.

- Contract with coach for the minimum amount of time.

- If at any time you start to feel uncomfortable with the way your coaching is going, tell your coach. You are the one who gets to design your coaching. You are the expert in your life, family and work. Coaching "holds a space" for *you* to sort, focus and decide.

How Can I Help? A Brief Coaching Exercise for Friends and Family

Family, friends and community, this section is for you

It takes a village to support a family impacted by autism. Many extended families, faith communities and neighbors ask "How can we help?" I'm so glad you asked!

Simply stated: friends and community support health.

An effective model of health under recent discussion (Ivey *et al.* 2005) focuses on five spheres crucial to personal wellness. And wellness contributes to both longevity and quality of life. The following list is a much-abbreviated version of their conclusions:

1. **creative sphere**—includes areas such as thinking, emotions, work, and positive humor

2. **coping**—leisure, stress management, self-worth, realistic beliefs

3. **social**—friendship, love

4. **essential**—spirituality, cultural identity, self-care

5. **physical**—exercise, nutrition.

Grandma, friend, uncle, neighbor, auntie, grandpa, faith-community teacher, which category jumps out at you?

Where are you most healthy in your life?

How can you utilize your own strengths to impact the autism-impacted family you know?

For example, if you ask your neighbor to join your daily two-mile walk, you're influencing the Physical Sphere. Or, if you email your sister 1500 miles away, describing her strengths as a mom and cheering her on, you're influencing the Coping Sphere and particularly her self-worth.

Possibly you are a co-worker in a team with the dad of a kid with autism. How can your positive sense of humor impact his Creative Sphere? Supporting health doesn't always have to be about the disability itself.

Perhaps you keep an immaculate, empty-nest house. How about donating an afternoon a week? (I had a friend do this for me during a particularly stressful time in our family's history. To this day, the scent of Pine-Sol smells like friendship.)

Not every person can offer support in every sphere. But most people are able to offer occasional help in one or two areas. Don't start with a grandiose plan that will magically fill in all of the cracks.

Coaching exercise

Coach yourself by answering the following questions:

1. Where *can* you help?

2. What do you like to do?

3. What are your strengths?

4. Where are *you* most healthy?

5. What's right in front of you?

6. What else?

7. Knowing you, what might stop you?

8. What are you going to do?

9. When? Date: _____ Time: _____

10. How will you prepare?

11. When will you do it?

12. Who can hold you accountable to do what you want to do?

Ideas to take away with you

What's your "take-away" from coaching yourself through How Can I Help? Writing it down anchors the learning.

"Autism-ese" Glossary

Asperger's Syndrome—"Children diagnosed with Asperger's disorder have difficulty with social interactions and understanding unspoken social cues...." Characteristics of "an individual with Asperger's disorder may be characterized by social isolation and sometimes relatively eccentric behavior. For example, an individual may have an... area of interest which usually leaves no space for more age appropriate, typically developing interests. Some examples of interests include trains, electricity, and weather, ... door knobs, chili peppers, astronomy, or history. In addition, the individual may have impairments in two-sided social interaction and nonverbal communication. Individuals with Asperger's are often highly intelligent and highly verbal, and although their speech may be grammatically correct, their speech may sound peculiar due to abnormalities of inflection or fluency. Oftentimes, individuals with Asperger's disorder get into more trouble in school, exasperate teachers, and are the subject of bullying. Boys are four times as likely as girls to be diagnosed with Asperger's." (Autism Spectrum Institute at Illinois State University, 2009b)

Autism Spectrum Disorder *(definition 1)*—also known as "ASD" and Pervasive Developmental Disorders. Five different syndromes are found underneath this medical diagnosis "umbrella." (Criteria for diagnosis are in the DSM-IV-TR (*Diagnostic and Statistical Manual of Mental Disorders*, American Psychiatric Association 2000)):

1. **Autism**—also called "classic" autism. The official medical diagnosis is "autistic disorder."

2. **Asperger's Syndrome**—meets the same medical criteria as autism, without the speech and language delay.

3. **PDD.NOS**—"Pervasive Developmental Disorder Not Otherwise Specified"—a diagnosis given to a person who has some of the characteristics of autism, but not enough to meet the actual "autistic disorder" diagnosis. Frequently, professionals use PDD.NOS for a young child displaying autism spectrum behavior who is not yet old enough developmentally to be evaluated on the "social" aspect of the diagnosis.

4. **Rhett's Disorder**—"A unique developmental disorder that is first recognized in infancy and seen almost always in girls, but can be rarely seen in boys" (International Rhett Syndrome Foundation, 2008).

5. **Childhood Disintegrative Disorder**—"A condition far less common than autism in which children develop normally until age three or four, but then develop a severe loss of social, communication and other skills" (Mayo Clinic, 2008). Autism typically occurs at an earlier age and with a less dramatic loss in skill than childhood disintegrative disorder.

Autism Spectrum *(definition 2)*— Particularly for higher functioning autism and Asperger's Syndrome, some professionals use broader criteria, such as *The Gillberg diagnostic criteria for Asperger's Syndrome* (Gillberg, 1991). The wider measures may include individuals with a *flavor* of autism spectrum, where not all the medical criteria are met, but, for example, the social impairment is present. This growing way of conceptualizing autism widens the Spectrum "umbrella." (Writer's note: Even if the person doesn't meet the more stringent medical criteria, if the autism/Asperger's interventions work—*use them!* I often say, "There's a little bit of autism in all of us.") For more information see Tony Attwood's book *The Complete Guide to Asperger's Syndrome,* Jessica Kingsley Publishers, 2007.

ASD—acronym for **A**utism **S**pectrum **D**isorder; often used as an adjective to describe someone with autism as in "the ASD individual."

Aspie—a term used by many people with Asperger's Syndrome to affectionately call their comrades or themselves. Not to be used as derogatory.

Classic autism—another term for "Autistic Spectrum Disorder." Not to be confused with Asperger's or "high functioning" autism. Official diagnosis is made by professionals (physicians, psychologists, psychiatrists, etc.) according to set criteria listed in the *Diagnostic and Statistical Manual (DSM-IV)*. Some symptoms include:

- limited eye contact, inappropriate facial expressions and emotional responses, avoidance of physical contact

- delayed speech without communicative gesturing (e.g. pointing), inability to engage in conversation, lack of pretend play

- inflexible routines, preoccupation with abnormal interests or parts/ functioning of objects, repetitive movements (e.g. hand flapping or wringing)

- onset of at least one symptom before age three (Autism Spectrum Institute at Illinois State University, 2009a).

DSM-IV-TR—Diagnostic and Statistical Manual of Mental Disorders, 4th edition, (2000), published by the American Psychiatric Association. This book is the official manual used by medical doctors, psychologists, therapists and counselors to diagnose mental illnesses. Although autism is a neurological disorder, the official diagnostic criteria are in the DSM-IV.

Educational label—sometimes incorrectly called an "educational *diagnosis*". In the state of Oregon, a child can have an educational label of autism or Asperger's without meeting the criteria for a medical diagnosis. Confusing? Yes, because the diagnostic criteria used are different. Most often, it is recommended that parents seek testing from both their local educational service district for the educational label and from a developmental pediatrician, psychologist or autism clinic for the medical diagnosis.

IEP—Individual Educational Plan.

Meltdown—the sudden and sometimes unexplainable outburst or shutdown of a person impacted by autism/Asperger's. The rapidly developing situation can lead to uncontrollable crying, self-injurious behavior, complete withdrawal and/or utter parent fatigue.

NT—See **Neurotypical**.

Neurotypical—a clinical word describing people not on the autism spectrum and meaning typical neurological development. "NT" is also used. For example, when visiting an Asperger's Adult Support Group, I was greeted by a member saying, "You're NT aren't you?"

OT—Occupational Therapy.

PT—Physical Therapy.

Person-centered—term used by many in the autism community to avoid labeling a person as "autistic." The preferred phrase is "person with autism," hence *person*-centered. The essential philosophy holds that people are people first and the label comes second. In the medical community, however, official diagnosis is described as "autistic disorder." When a doctor or clinic uses this terminology, the intent is not to offend or label, but rather to perform their job of giving a medically accurate diagnosis.

Perseveration or **perseverate**—persistently repeating an activity or motion. For children with autism, perseveration can become problematic to the exclusion of other activities or interactions.

Refrigerator Mother Theory—an autism theory from the 1940s to 1960s attributing autism to a mother's "genuine lack of...warmth" toward their autistic children (Laidler 2004). The primary flaw in the theory is that many mothers also have other children without autistic features. In the past 20 years, research has overwhelmingly de-bunked the "Refrigerator Mom Theory."

Sensory issues—"Sensory integration problems stem from the brain's ability to process correctly information received through...senses of taste, touch, smell, sight and sound. People can be hyposensitive in some areas (meaning they fail to pick up cues) and hypersensitive in others (meaning they are overly sensitive to stimulation of a sense)... When a person's senses are over- or understimulated, it affects their behaviour as they try to compensate..." (Sicile-Kira 2004, p 266). Some behaviors might include flapping hands or fingers, plugging ears, pacing, squealing, self-injury, etc.

Short bus—an expression describing the small yellow buses used in many places to transport special needs children.

Spectrum—a shortcut for Autism Spectrum Disorder, for example "She's on spectrum."

Speech—often used as a shortcut for Speech Therapy, for example "He has speech today."

Stim, stims or stimming—short for self-stimulation. Many parents and professionals use "stim" to describe behavior such as rocking, flapping, tapping, pacing, playing with a fidget toy, etc. Example: "She sure was stimming in group a lot today."

International Resources

Autism Coaching

Cope to Hope Coaching

www.copetohope.com

Ruth's private coaching practice, "Joining Asperger's/autism-impacted families and individuals to move from just coping to hoping." The highly effective method of phone-coaching makes the world a little smaller.

Australia Resources

Autism Info Australia

www.autisminfo.org.au

"At Autism Info Australia, our mission is simple – we want to provide clear information for parents on what ASD means and outline some of the services and treatments available today in Australia." (Autism Info Australia, 2009)

Tony Attwood (resource title)

www.tonyattwood.com/au

A world renowned expert in Asperger's/autism :"From my clinical experience I consider that children and adults with Asperger's Syndrome have a different, not defective, way of thinking." (Attwood, 2009)

Canada Resources

Autism Canada Foundation

www.autismcanada.org

"We felt there was a lack of representation, in Canada, of all effective treatments and therapies for autism. We decided that Canada needed an organization that provided 'uncensored' resources to parents and caregivers, with special emphasis on biomedical treatments." (Autism Canada Foundation, 2009)

Autism Today

www.autismtoday.com

"With our broad database of highly interactive members, we are an excellent established vehicle to conduct surveys and find interested participants for research projects and educational training." (Autism Today, 1998-2009)

New Zealand Resources

Autism New Zealand, Inc.

www.autismnz.org.nz

"…[P]rovided support, training advocacy, resources and information on autism spectrum disorders including Asperger's syndrome. Our members include those who have these conditions, their family/whanau, caregivers and professionals working with them." (Autism New Zealand, Inc, 2009)

South Africa Resources

Autism South Africa

www.autismsouthafrica.org

Provides a wide variety of services including "parent and professional support and guidance" while distributing information, facilitating and supporting grassroot services in underserved areas and encouraging and assisting with autism-specific research.

Autism Western Cape

www.autismwesterncape.or

"A part of our world, not a world apart...In 2003, the Society for Autistic Children was restructured into a new legal structure, governed by an independent Board of Directors with the emphasis of providing services based on sound business principles, working in close collaboration with Government Departments and partners in the disability sector and private sector." (Autism Western Cape, 2009)

United Kingdom Resources

The National Autistic Society

www.nas.org.uk

"We offer a range of information services for people with ASDs, families and professionals. These include our UK-wide Autism Services Directory, professional research tools and an online shop selling books, leaflets, videos, DVDs and CD-ROMs." (National Autistic Society, 2009)

Autism Independent UK®

www.autismuk.com

Formerly known as ®Society For The Autistically Handicapped. "[E]xists to increase awareness of autism, together with well established and newly developed approaches in the diagnosis, assessment, education and treatment. The main goal is to improve the quality of life for persons with Autism." (Autism Independent UK, 2009)

The Asperger's Syndrome Foundation

www.apsergerfoundation.org.uk

[C]ommitted to promoting awareness and understanding of Asperger's Syndrome. The Foundation aims to promote high quality support and services, and to enable people with Asperger's syndrome to develop into members of the community who are respected for their contribution and recognised for their unique differences." (The Asperger's Syndrome Foundation, 2009)

United States Resources

Autism Society of America

www.autism-society.org

From their website "ASA...exists to improve the lives of all affected by autism....by increasing public awareness about the day-to-day issues faced by people on the spectrum, advocating for appropriate services for individuals across the lifespan, and providing the latest information regarding treatment, education, research and advocacy ."

ARC of the United States

www.thearc.org

"The Arc is the world's largest community based organization of and for people with intellectual and developmental disabilities provid[ing] an array of services and support for families and individual chapters..." (The ARC of the United States, 2009)

Autism Speaks

www.autismspeaks.org

"Autism Speaks aims to bring the autism community together as one strong voice to urge the government and private sector to listen to our concerns and take action to address this urgent global health crisis."

Disability in the Family

www.disabilityinthefamily.com

Lisa Lieberman provides "Tools for navigating the emotional journey" of raising a child with a disability.

Social Thinking

www.socialthinking.com

Michelle Garcia Winner's methodology is particularly effective for individuals with higher-functioning forms of autism spectrum disorders, such as Asperger Syndrome.

References

American Heritage® Dictionary of the English Language, 4th edn (2006) Boston, MA: Houghton Mifflin. Available at http://dictionary.reference.com/browse/meltdown, accessed on 22 January 2009.

Attwood, T. (2007) *The Complete Guide to Asperger's Syndrome*. London: Jessica Kingsley Publishers.

Autism Spectrum Institute at Illinois State University (2009a). *www.autismspectrum.ilstu.edu*. Accessed 28 February 2009, from www.IllinoisState.edu: www.autismspectrum.ilstu.edu/autism/classicautism.shtml

Autism Spectrum Institute at Illinois State University (2009b). *www.autismspectrum.ilstu.edu*. Accessed 2 March 2009, from www.IllinoisState.edu: www.autismspectrum.ilstu.edu/autism/aspergersdisorder.shtml

Bolman, W. M. (2006) 'The Autistic Family Life Cycle: Family, Stress and Divorce.' Autism Society of America National Conference. Providence, Rhode Island: ASA Online Archives. Accessed 5 May 2009 from http://asastore.confex.com/asastore/

Creswell, J., Miller, L., & Thomas, L. (2005 June) 'How Do I Know if I'm Ready for a Coach?' Quiz. *Class Curriculum, Introduction to Coaching*, 1. Portland, OR: Western Seminary.

DeMyer, M., Hingtgen, J. and Jackson, R. (1981) 'Infantile autism reviewed: a decade of research.' *Schizophrenic Bulletin 7*, 388–451.

Fletcher, J. (1993) *Patterns of High Performance*. San Francisco, CA: Berrett-Kohler Publishers.

Fox, J. (2008) *Your Child's Strengths*. New York, NY: Penguin Group.

Gallup Organization (2007) *Clifton Youth StrengthsExplorer*, 2nd edn. Princeton, NJ: The Gallup Organization. Available at www.strengthsexplorer.com, accessed 30 January 2009.

Gillberg, C. (1991) *Autism and Asperger's Syndrome*. (ed.U. Frith) Cambridge: Cambridge University Press.

Gottman, J.M. (1999) *The Seven Principles for Making Marriage Work*. Seattle, WA: Random House.

Gottman, J.M. (2004) *Marital Therapy: A Research-Based Approach Clinicians Manual*. Seattle, WA: The Gottman Institute.

International Rhett Syndrome Foundation (2008) *Rhett Syndrome Fact Sheet*. Accessed 13 March 2009, from www.rhettsyndrome.org: www.rettsyndrome.org/index.php?option=com_content&task=blogsection&id=4&Itemid=375

Isbell, D. (2008, November 25) Interview with R. Knott Schroeder.

Ivey, A., Ivey, M., Myers, J. and Sweeney, T. (2005) *Developmental Counseling and Therapy: Promoting Wellness Over the Lifespan*. Boston, MA: Houghton Mifflin.

Knopf, G. (2000, May) Interview with R. Knott Schroeder.

Kogan, M. D., Strickland, B. B., Blimberg, S. J., Singh, G. K., Perrin, J. M. and van Dyck, P. C. (2008) 'A national profile of the health care experiences and family impact of autism spectrum disorder among children in the United States, 2005–2006.' *Pediatrics 122*, December, e1149–1158. Available at www.pediatrics.org/cgi/content/full/122/6/e1149, accessed 30 January 2009.

Laidler, M. J. (2004) *"The Refrigerator Mother" Hypothesis of Autism*. Autism Watch. Available at www.autism-watch.org/causes/rm.shtml, accessed 30 January 2009.

Lee, L. (2006) *Autism: Living with my Brother Tiger*. Salem, OR: Special Needs Publishing.

Lieberman, L. (2005) *A 'Stranger' Among Us: Hiring In-Home Support for a Child with Autism Spectrum Disorders or Other Neurological Differences*. Shawnee Mission, KS: Autism Asperger Publishing Company.

Martindale, E. (2008a) *Restoration and Rejuvenation. Group Therapy Handout*. Portland, OR.

Martindale, E. (2008b) ROLF. *Group Therapy Handouts*. Portland, OR.

Martindale, E. (2008c) *Soothing and Comforting Activities. Group Therapy Handouts*. Portland, OR.

Mayo Clinic (2008) *Children's Health.* Accessed 19 March 2009, from www. mayoclinic.com: www.mayoclinic.com/health/childhood-disintegrative-disorder/DS00801

Ming, X., Sun, Y.-M., Nachajon, R. V., Brimacombe, M. and Walters, A. S. (2009) 'Prevalence of Parasomnia in Autistic Children with Sleep Disorders' (Provisional PDF). *Clinical Medicine Pediatrics, 3,* 1–10.

Montes, G. and Halterman, J. S. (2008a) 'Association of childhood autism spectrum disorders and loss of family income.' *Pediatrics 121,* April, e821–e826. Available at www.pediatrics.org/cgi/content/full/121/4/e821, accessed 30 January 2009.

Montes, G. and Halterman, J. S. (2008b) 'Childcare problems and employment among families with preschool-aged children with autism in the United States.' *Pediatrics 122,* July, e202–e208. Available at www.pediatrics.org/cgi/content/full/122/1/e202, accessed 22 January 2009.

Parish, P. (1976) *Good Work, Amelia Bedelia.* New York, NY: Avon Books.

Random House, Inc. (2008) *Dictionary.com Unabridged (v1.1).* Available at http://dictionary.reference.com, accessed 30 January 2009.

Rath, T. (2007) *StrengthsFinder 2.0.* New York, NY: Gallup Press.

Sicile-Kira, C. (2004) Autism Spectrum Disorders. New York, NY: Penguin.

Siegel, B. and Silverstein, S. (1994) *What About Me?: Growing Up with a Developmentally Disabled Sibling.* Cambridge, MA: Perseus Publishing.

Wenzel, D. M. (2008, November 12) Interview with R. Knott Schroeder.

Whitworth, L. Kimsey-House, H. and Sandahl, P. (1998) *Co-Active Coaching.* Mountain View, CA: Davies-Black Publishing.

Index